MEDIA MISCHIEF and MISDEEDS

REGNERY GATEWAY

REED IRVINE
Chairman, Accuracy in Media

● CHICAGO

For further information about
ACCURACY IN MEDIA, contact
Reed Irvine at:
1275 K Street, NW, Suite 1150
Washington, DC 20005
Phone: (202) 371-6710

The author would like to thank the *Colorado Springs Sun,*
the *Santa Ana Register,* the *Journal Herald* of Dayton, Ohio,
and Bob Englehart for their kind permission to reprint the
cartoon illustrations in this book.

Published by Regnery Gateway, Inc.
360 West Superior Street
Chicago, Illinois 60610

Manufactured in the United States of America.

ISBN: 0-89526-606-7

CONTENTS

PREFACE

I launched on a career of media criticism in 1969, when disgust with the media—particularly television, for pouring gasoline on the flames of riots in our cities and turmoil on our campuses—propelled me, together with a few friends, into founding Accuracy in Media. At the time I was an official in the Division of International Finance of the Federal Reserve Board in Washington. My connection with journalism was strictly that of a consumer of its products. Like many others during the late 1960s, I had come face to face with many serious defects in what the journalists were churning out.

I had written many letters to editors and broadcasters pointing out serious errors and distortions. I had written the presidents of the television network news departments urging that they create their own self-policing organization to guard against the kinds of abuses that characterized their coverage of such events as the riots in Chicago at the time of the 1968 Democratic National Convention. They weren't interested. I tried to find someone in the journalistic profession who would be willing to head up an organization that would bring some systematic moral suasion to bear on our increasingly powerful media by administering responsible, systematic criticism.

Arthur Krock, the venerable retired Washington bureau chief of the *New York Times,* struck me as being the ideal person for such an assignment. He was respected in the profession, and criticisms coming from him would obviously carry a lot of weight. Mr. Krock declined the honor. He explained to me that the *New York Times* would necessarily be one of the targets of such an organization and that his continuing ties with the *Times* precluded his engaging in any public criticism of that paper.

This brought me to the realization that the type of organization I had in mind would have to be representative of and run by consumers of the journalistic product, not by the producers. The reporters, editors and broadcasters simply could not be expected to criticize each other without pulling their punches. They were friends, or they were indebted to each other, or they were afraid that they or their good friends might become the targets of criticism in retaliation for any criticism they might mete out.

That was why we created Accuracy in Media with the deliberate policy of not involving active journalists in its work or its direction. We started with $200 contributed by a good friend, Wilson C. Lucom, in September 1969. The announcement was not greeted with any visible fear and trembling on the part of the media. Indeed, they took no notice of it whatsoever. A few weeks later they were rocked by the speech that Vice President Spiro Agnew delivered in Des Moines, Iowa in which he excoriated the media for their mischief and misdeeds. Agnew's speech was as much a surprise to me as to everyone else. It had no connection with AIM, but the favorable public response to his attack on the media confirmed my own feeling that the time was ripe for our little project.

How do you go about taking on such powerful media giants as ABC, CBS, NBC, the *New York Times* and the *Washington Post* with nothing but $200 and a typewriter in your basement that you can bang away at only on nights and weekends? I took inspiration from these lines from Shakespeare:

Thrice is he armed that hath his quarrel just,

And he but naked, though locked up in steel,
Whose conscience with injustice is corrupted.

I naively thought that if Accuracy in Media's criticisms were just, accurate and well documented, we would be able to prevail over those who were responsible for unfair and inaccurate reporting. Surely in those great media institutions we would be able to find men and women who would see the justice of our complaints and who would insist that corrections be made and remedial action taken to prevent repetitions of the flawed reporting.

It didn't work that way. I concluded before long that there were a lot of consciences corrupted with injustice in the news business. While they were willing to mouth their devotion to truth and accuracy, they tended to follow the practice of standing by their stories even when they were manifestly wrong. It was very difficult in many cases to find any consciences in those powerful media organizations that could be pricked with a pen.

After a few years, I came to realize that what was needed was a medium by which my criticisms could be brought to public attention without depending on the conscience and good will of the newspaper, magazine or broadcaster that I was criticizing. In 1972, AIM began publishing its newsletter, the *AIM Report:* by the end of 1983 circulation was over 30,000. In 1976, I began my weekly syndicated newspaper column, "Accuracy in Media." It was picked up by some 100 newspapers around the country, mostly papers with a relatively small circulation. Nevertheless, in aggregate, this gave our criticism a potential audience of a couple of million people. A few years later, we began a daily radio commentary, and in 1981, with the help of the Allied Educational Foundation, we launched a speakers bureau which was soon blanketing the country with AIM speakers. We delivered 500 talks in 1983.

The media's antipathy to hard-hitting, factual criticism of their misdeeds and mischief has not measurably abated since 1969. What I call Big Media—the television networks, the newspapers with national influence, the news magazines and the wire services have not been eager to run stories about the criticisms that I have directed against them in the *AIM Report,* my column and on our radio program. But like the steady dripping of water that wears away granite, our criticism has had an effect.

In 1983, the media felt the sting of the negative public reaction to their arrogance and claims of special privilege as never before. John Chancellor, the NBC News editorial commentator, suffered a double shock. First, he was shocked when the government didn't permit reporters to cover the Grenada rescue operation for the first 48 hours, and he said so on the air. Then he was shocked when he was inundated with mail from his viewers, who overwhelmingly disagreed with his criticism. He was not the only one.

Time magazine devoted the cover story in its December 12 issue to the public's negative feelings about the media. In its catalog of criticisms of journalists it included this: "They are arrogant and self-righteous, brushing aside most criticism as the uninformed carping of cranks and ideologues." This book is a collection of some that criticism they brushed aside—the columns I published in 1983. I want to pay my respects to all those editors and publishers who had the courage and decency to run them. May their tribe increase! For the media are too powerful and too important to function in our society without at least the restraint that this kind of hard-hitting criticism can impose. They, like all other institutions, are vulnerable to the corruption that comes with too much power.

Reed Irvine
Chairman
Accuracy in Media, Inc.

NEWS ITEM: ABC NEWS & WASHINGTON POST POLL SHOWS MOST AMERICANS BELIEVE THAT POVERTY AND LACK OF RESPECT OF HUMAN RIGHTS ARE A GREATER CAUSE OF UNREST THAN SUBVERSION!

1

The Missing Side of the Legal Services Story

In mid-December, the *Washington Post* stirred up a storm about the fees and expenses collected by the members of the board of directors of the Legal Services Corporation. The first blast came on December 15, when the *Post* ran a front-page story under the headline, "Legal Service Appointees Get Fat Fees." The story pointed out that the directors of this federally funded corporation had collected consulting fees totaling $156,201 during the first 11 months of 1982, compared to $72,029 for all of 1981. The article noted that directors have always been entitled to collect consulting fees for the time they work, but it suggested that the directors appointed by President Reagan had been abusing this provision.

The *Washington Post* followed up this story the following day with another page one article headlined "Legal Services Head's Contract Sweet." The story charged that the new president of the Legal Services Corporation, Donald P. Bogard, had been given a contract that provides for extraordinary fringe benefits. These included a provision for severance pay amounting to a year's salary if Mr. Bogard were dismissed from his job, payment of fees for membership in a private club, living expenses in Washington and two trips a month to his home in Indianapolis until June 15, 1983. The latter provisions were included because Mr. Bogard did not want to move his family to Washington before the end of the school year.

The *Post* followed up the next day with a page-two story saying that President Reagan had asked the Office of Management and Budget to investigate the "large consulting fees charged by the board of the Legal Services Corporation." It followed this the next day with another front-page story saying that a congressman was going to ask that federal prosecutors act to recover the money paid to the board members on the ground that the payments had been illegal.

Members of Congress, the public and the press were outraged by these revelations that made it appear that the Reagan appointees to the board were ripping off the Treasury. But the stories were actually another journalistic atrocity on the part of the *Washington Post*. Indeed, some members of the Legal Services Corporation board suspect that the *Post* sought to create a phony scandal in order to help secure the passage of an amendment introduced by Sen. Lowell Weicker to keep the Reagan appointees on the board from carrying out their program of halting the waste and misuse of the $240 million annual budget of the Legal Services Corporation.

If that was the intent, the *Post* succeeded. The Weicker amendment, which tied the hands of the board in altering the spending pattern developed by the Carter board, passed. It requires the board to make the same grants in the same amounts as were made by the previous board even though it has evidence that many of those grants were wasteful or were used illegally. While the *Washington Post* was front-paging false charges that the Reagan board had ripped off the Treasury to the tune of about $80,000, it was silent about the millions of dollars that would be misused and wasted as a result of the passage of the Weicker amendment. There is reason to believe that amendment passed in the lame duck session of Congress only because of the furor over board fees and expenses created by the *Washington Post*.

Was the furor justified? Not at all. It turned out that the

higher fees and expenses paid to the new board reflected the fact that it was holding many more meetings and putting in a lot more time than had the previous board. It held 28 meetings in 1982 compared to only 12 meetings held in 1981. Dividing the total paid in fees and expenses to the board members by the number of meetings held, we find that the average cost per meeting in 1982 was nearly $2,000 below the average cost in 1981. That was despite the fact that Congress had authorized a 15% increase in the per diem fees paid to board members.

The fuss over the contract of Donald Bogard, the new president of Legal Services Corporation, was equally phony. It was very similar to the contracts given to his predecessors, with one easily justifiable difference. The *Post* stories were dishonest.

January 7, 1983

2

The Media Ahead of Reagan on the Andropov Scandal

The media were slow in getting onto the story of the evidence that Soviet dictator Yuri Andropov was involved in the May 1981 attempt to murder Pope John Paul II, but they have been catching up. *Newsweek* magazine finally got around to making the plot to kill the Pope its cover story for its January 3, 1983 issue. *Newsweek* quoted the Italian Minister of Justice, Clelio Darida, as saying that Mehmet Ali Agca, the gunman who shot the Pope, "operated in close contact with the Bulgarians."

The magazine said, "Last week the Italian government threw its weight behind the theory that Moscow wanted the outspoken John Paul killed to prevent him from interfering in Polish affairs." It noted that the Italian Minister of Defense, Lelio Lagoria, a socialist, had said, "Ali Agca's attack on the Pope is to be considered as a real act of war in a time of peace, a precautionary and alternative solution to the invasion of Poland."

Newsweek claimed that a high ranking Vatican source had told them, "From the very beginning, (we were) absolutely convinced that the KGB was behind the plot. Now it turns out to be right." On December 29, 1982, the Soviets provided some confirmation of the theory that they launched the attack on the Pope because of their concern about his influence in Poland. The official news agency, Tass, distributed a vicious attack on Pope John Paul II, asserting that under his leadership the Vatican had been involved in "subversive" activities in Poland and "anti-communist propaganda on a vast scale." It said that Solidarity, the popular Polish union that had been such a thorn in the side of the communists, "was born...in the Catholic Church."

While elements of the media, notably the *New York Times,* have lagged behind in exposing the Soviet role in the attempt to rid themselves of this potent enemy, the evidence has proven to be persuasive to such distinguished foreign policy experts as former Secretary of State Henry Kissinger and former National Security Adviser Zbigniew Brzezinski, as well as to former CIA Director Richard Helms. Kissinger said on Cable News Network on December 30, that Helms had told him that the attack on the Pope "had all the earmarks of a KGB operation." Kissinger added, "It had to be the Soviets. The Bulgarians have no interest in coming after the Pope."

Brzezinski gave an interview to an Italian paper, *La Stampa,* which was published December 30, in which he said: "There is no doubt that the investigation made by Italian authorities has established the complicity of Bulgaria in the attack against the Pope. Those who know the reality of eastern Europe automatically deduce that the Soviet Union was in command of the operation." Brzezinski termed the attack on the Pope "the most monumental assassination attempt carried out in this century."

The United States government has lagged far behind the media and these former high officials in taking cognizance of the evidence that Yuri Andropov has the blood of Pope John Paul II on his hands. Columnist William Safire of the *New York Times* has reported that our Central Intelligence Agency has deprecated the evidence amassed by the Italians. This may help to explain the footdragging on the part of the *New York Times,* which in both its news stories and in one astonishing editorial has tried to downplay the charges of Bulgarian and Soviet involvement in the plot. I suspect that Henry Kamm, the *Times* correspondent in Rome, has been more influenced by the American embassy than by the Italian authorities.

The White House and the State Department have refused to make any comment on the matter. President Reagan was asked about it by Hedrick Smith of the *New York Times* at his January 5 news conference. The President ducked the question, saying that as long as the Italians were investigating it would not be proper for him to comment.

That is strange, because the Italian cabinet ministers have not felt constrained to avoid comment. If the shoe were on the other foot, the Soviets would have quickly mounted a massive campaign to destroy Reagan. The timidity of our leaders must amuse them.

January 14, 1983

3

The Capitol Hill Cocaine Cover-Up

Do you remember the cocaine scandal that erupted on Capitol Hill in 1982? It was overshadowed at the time by charges that members of Congress were involved in homosexual relations with some Capitol pages. The homosexual scandal has since been laid to rest, with a finding that the charges made by a couple of former pages were untrue. No such finding has been made with respect to the charge that some members of the House and Senate were users of cocaine, but the matter seemed to drop out of sight.

However, the scandal surfaced again on January 6, when NBC correspondent Brian Ross reported on the NBC Nightly News that a federal grand jury had just heard testimony about allegations of cocaine deliveries and use right off the floor of the House of Representatives. Ross said that federal investigators had been told that cocaine had been brought into the Democratic cloakroom, a lounge off the House floor for Democratic members of Congress.

Brian Ross interviewed a police detective named Michael

Hubbard who began the investigation of drug use on Capitol Hill in April 1981. Hubbard used the office of former Congressman Robert Dornan as a base for his undercover work. His investigation culminated a year later, in April 1982, in the arrest of Douglas Marshall, a former Carter White House intern and the son of Sylvan Marshall, a prominent Washington lawyer. Douglas Marshall was arrested in his father's home. Mr. Hubbard said that he was caught with cocaine valued at $250,000. He confessed to being a drug dealer, and he said that his clients included a number of congressmen and senators, some of whom he named.

Only one name surfaced in the media, that of Congressman Barry Goldwater, Jr. Detective Hubbard said on the NBC News program that the investigation could have explored drug use by a dozen or more members of Congress. He said that the investigation had not been pursued aggressively by the U.S. Attorney's office and the Justice Department and that valuable time had been lost. In fact, he said that Daniel Bernstein of the U.S. Attorney's office had actually dropped the charges against Douglas Marshall, permitting the confessed drug dealer to legally leave the country. Hubbard said that the prosecutors were not interested in going after the members of Congress who were Marshall's drug customers. He said he had no doubt that cocaine was still being sold on Capitol Hill.

Last November the Justice Department got the grand jury to indict Douglas Marshall on charges of conspiracy to distribute cocaine, but by then Marshall was in Sydney, Australia. Interviewed on the Braden-Buchanan radio talk show in Washington on January 7, detective Hubbard said he didn't know of any efforts being made to have Marshall extradited. His former customers are surely hoping that Marshall will stay put in Australia until the whole thing blows over.

At this moment the chances that it will be covered up seem rather good. The *New York Times* reported January 6 that some people in the Justice Department think that the Department should not go after members of Congress who use drugs. They say that since the federal government does not normally prosecute drug users, it ought not to treat members of Congress differently. They said they would favor prosecution only if the

Congressmen were regular users, dealers or were using staff to get their drugs. That was not the position taken when a special prosecutor investigated charges that White House aides Hamilton Jordan and Tim Kraft had used cocaine during the Carter administration. The attitude then was that public officials ought to be held to higher standards than ordinary citizens. I think the public would be especially angry about a cover-up for members of Congress at a time when the President is pressing for a crackdown on drugs.

But important elements of the media are going along with the cover-up. The *Washington Post*, the *Washington Times*, ABC and CBS have been mute. The *New York Times*, NBC, UPI, the Braden-Buchanan shows on Cable News Network and WRC radio, and the *Washington Inquirer* deserve a lot of credit for exposing the footdragging by the Justice Department.

January 21, 1983

4

Phil Donahue Plays Fair

Having been engaged in criticizing the media for over a decade, I have learned that not many journalists react to criticism with enthusiasm or even grace. I have had the suave anchorman of the CBS Evening News, Dan Rather, and the scholarly columnist, Joe Kraft, throw unprintable expletives at me and hang up the phone. Ben Bradlee, the distinguished executive editor of the *Washington Post,* once sent me a note in which he called me "a miserable, carping, retromingent vigilante." That four-syllable word has to do with the urinary function. I have had to fight to get papers like the *Washington Post* and *New York Times* to publish letters pointing out serious errors that they had made. My organization, Accuracy in Media, has at times had difficulty even in getting these papers to sell us space to publicize the criticisms that they should have printed for nothing.

Until very recently, I had thought of the popular talk-show host, Phil Donahue, as just one more of these thin-skinned media types who was good at dishing out criticism but resentful of anyone who criticized him. I am writing this column to point out that Phil Donahue has proven himself to be a far better man than I had previously thought.

Last October, the *AIM Report*, the newsletter published by Accuracy in Media, carried an article by author Victor Lasky that was very critical of Phil Donahue and his program. Lasky charged that Donahue had been indoctrinating his huge national audience with his own liberal political and social philosophy. He said that the "new vistas" that Donahue opened up for the millions of housewives who watch his daily program "generally consist of views which can only be described as knee-jerk liberal on subjects ranging from politics to every variety of sexual perversity known to humankind." The article went on to document that contention with examples from a number of Donahue programs.

It was as tough a criticism as Accuracy in Media has directed at any prominent figure in the profession. I am sure that it made Donahue mad. We appended to Lasky's article a note urging the readers to write to Donahue's sponsors, telling them what they thought of his program, and we even offered to send them free a publication that would enable them to find the name and address of any company whose products they saw advertised on television. That was to make it easier for them to communicate with the sponsors.

Instead of receiving an angry letter of complaint from Phil Donahue or anyone connected with his program, we received an invitation for Vic Lasky and myself to appear on his show! Quite frankly, I was astonished. I had never before experienced that response from someone we had criticized.

We accepted the invitation, but I suspected that Mr. Donahue might be trying to lay some kind of trap for us. Would he not try to get even by seeing if he could dig up something that he could use on national television to embarrass or hurt us? That has been tried by other journalists who have felt the sting of our criticisms.

My suspicions about Phil Donahue proved to be totally unfounded. He was a gracious and even generous host. He had no dirty tricks up his sleeve. He discussed the article that Victor Lasky had written about him, joking that he was hurt because

Lasky had written several books attacking such figures as John F. Kennedy and his brother, Robert, but he had devoted only an article to Phil Donahue. He gave us and the third guest on the program, the Rev. Jerry Falwell, an opportunity to state our criticisms of the media in general and of his show in particular. He told his audience about Accuracy in Media's newsletter, the *AIM Report,* and gave them the address to which to write. He even told them about that sponsors' guide and how they could get a copy. (Write to AIM, 1275 K St., N. W., Washington, D. C. 20005, sending a stamped, self-addressed #10 envelope.)

It took a big man to do what Phil Donahue did in having two of his severest critics appear on his program. He said on the air that "the big brass" were terrified about his doing the program. For one thing, I guess, they didn't want to see the members of the audience encouraged to write to the advertisers. Phil Donahue is one gutsy guy.

January 28, 1983

5

Media Expose the Tarnish on Halos of Church Councils

The National Council of Churches and the World Council of Churches (NCC and WCC) were the targets of a media double whammy in January. To the great surprise of many of its critics, including this one, "60 Minutes" aired an expose of the NCC and WCC on January 23 that revealed a lot of tarnish on the halos of these two controversial groups. This followed publication in the January issue of *Reader's Digest* of a hardhitting article criticizing the NCC for strong political tilt to the left.

These charges are not new, but they had not previously been so forcefully presented on a widely-viewed network television program or in a mass circulation magazine. The thrust of the *Reader's Digest* article by Rael Jean Isaac was that a significant amount of money contributed by American churchgoers is finding its way to political organizations that include "groups supporting the Palestine Liberation Organization, the governments of Cuba and Vietnam, and the pro-Soviet totalitarian movements of Latin America, Asia and Africa, and several violence-prone fringe groups in the United States."

Mrs. Isaac cited the activities of the National Council of Churches as an example of what is going on, unbeknownst to most of those who are putting up the dollars. She pointed out that in 1979-81, the president of the NCC, the Rev. M. William Howard, embarked on a program to publicize "political prisoners" in the United States. He visited prisoners around the country that he claimed were jailed for political reasons, such as Larry Jackson, a black convicted of murder, who was involved with an organization that wants to convert five southern states into an independent "black republic." In choosing which prisoners to visit, Howard was guided by the research of an organization affiliated with a Soviet front group called the International Association of Democratic Lawyers.

The *Reader's Digest* article pointed out that James Armstrong, the current president of the NCC had defended the communist government of Vietnam after many former anti-war activists, headed by Joan Baez, had criticized it for the oppression that gave rise to the "boat people." She said that the Church World Service, which receives about 70 percent of the NCC's budget, gave nearly half a million dollars to communist Vietnam to help with its "New Economic Zones," the areas to which the communists exiled people they didn't like.

"60 Minutes" buttressed much that *Reader's Digest* said about the NCC. Morley Safer, the correspondent, interviewed NCC President James Armstrong. He asked him about the NCC's funding of the Cuban Resource Center, an outfit that has published booklets glorifying Castro's communist regime in Cuba. Bishop Armstrong claimed to know nothing about that, saying, "My responsibility here is not to dig into corners and into closets, but to do things I consider most important." I imagine that most of those who contribute their hard-earned dollars to the NCC would agree that it is important to see that their money is not used to finance propaganda for communist regimes that oppress and persecute Christians.

Morley Safer brought up the support the NCC gives to the World Council of Churches. He cited a booklet by the WCC which said: "The international capitalist economic system is repugnant to the concept of justice and is a denial of the lordship of Christ and therefore an abomination." He asked Armstrong if he agreed with that. Armstrong said he did not, but he qualified that. He said the National Council of Churches "does not belong to Karl Marx and we don't belong to Adam Smith," referring to the father of free market economics.

Safer also interviewed the secretary general of the World Council of Churches, who showed his ideological colors by trying to deny that communist East Germany is a country surrounded by barbed wire to keep its people from escaping. He acknowledged that WCC money had been given to terrorists in Africa who had murdered Christian missionaries. He defended the grants, saying they had not been given to pay for weapons.

The NCC has expressed outrage at both the *Reader's Digest* article and the "60 Minutes" program, but its statements fail to refute the specific evidence showing that its tilt is far more in the direction of Karl Marx than Adam Smith.

February 4, 1983

6

Paranoia Hits CBS News

Van Gordon Sauter, president of CBS News, recently gave a speech in which he spoke darkly of groups that are engaging in "a search and destroy mission against the media." Sauter said these groups are using Gen. William C. Westmoreland's $120 million libel suit against CBS as "a rallying point for people who seek to use it as an instrument for damaging the image, spirit and aggressiveness of the news media."

Sauter said these people view "an independent, searching press as a threat to what they perceive as traditional values." He said, "They seek to diminish the voice—the calm, objective voice—of the media so they can advance their narrow agendas and shout above those who are committed only to fair and accurate reporting of controversial issues."

Asked who Mr. Sauter had in mind, Robert Chandler, senior vice president of CBS News, named Accuracy in Media, the organization which I head, and the American Legal Foundation. AIM has been a vigorous critic of the CBS program that gave rise to the Westmoreland libel suit since it was aired over a year ago. The American Legal Foundation recently filed a complaint with the Federal Communications Commission charging that CBS had violated the fairness doctrine in its treatment of the controversial issues involved in the Westmoreland documentary.

Mr. Sauter and Mr. Chandler and all their associates at CBS News know very well that the criticisms that we and others have leveled against the vicious documentary that impugned the integrity of Gen. Westmoreland are well-founded. They know it because they have in their possession a 61-page document known as the Benjamin report which spells out the unethical, dishonest conduct involved in the making of that documentary.

Mr. Sauter and his associates are keeping the Benjamin report secret. They are resisting the efforts of Gen. Westmoreland's attorneys to obtain it. They have resisted the effort of Accuracy in Media to let the CBS shareholders vote on a resolution asking that the Benjamin report be made available to them and to the public. They begged the Securities and Exchange Commission to okay their refusal to put the issue to a vote of the CBS shareholders.

Why the secrecy about this document that details the findings of a six-week investigation of how the Westmoreland documentary was planned, assembled and edited? Is there any doubt that if Burton Benjamin, the CBS News vice president who made that investigation, had given the producers a clean bill of health CBS would have released his report and distributed it far and wide?

The Benjamin report remains one of the deepest secrets of CBS News for one reason. It exposes the inaccuracy of Mr. Sauter's claim that the critics of CBS are attacking "the calm, objective voice of the media" that is "committed only to fair and accurate reporting of controversial issues." Even though I have not seen the report, I say that with assurance because of the way CBS has handled it. It has admitted that the producers did violate CBS News regulations. It has admitted that they should not have accused Gen. Westmoreland of leading a conspiracy. And Mr. Sauter himself refuses to declare publicly that the documentary was fair to General Westmoreland.

The latest excuse that Mr. Sauter has given for not releasing the Benjamin report is that "those who contributed to it were told they would do so in confidence." Mr. Sauter says that "confidentiality is imperative if news organizations are going to conduct exacting post-broadcast or post-publication studies of their own work."

That is absurd. Benjamin was assigned to investigate serious charges of wrongdoing on the part of CBS News personnel. To promise them all confidentiality would spell "whitewash" from the beginning. Those of us who have put the heat on CBS to release the report are not trying to destroy the media. We are trying to protect it from those in the media who discredit their profession by their deeds and by covering up for others.

February 11, 1983

7

Churches' Rebuttal of "60 Minutes" Flawed

The National Council of Churches and its mainline member churches were infuriated by the program aired about them and the World Council of Churches on the CBS program, "60 Minutes," on January 23. The program charged that the NCC and WCC, while doing much good work in the world, were also aiding Marxist causes by giving them money and helping spread their propaganda.

The churches have responded with denials and demands for air time to respond to the charges. They have said that CBS should have said a great deal more about their religious and charitable works, and they have pointed to what they say are inaccuracies in the case that was made against them.

In my view, "60 Minutes" made it abundantly clear that it recognized that these church groups were doing many admirable things in the world and that the activities discussed on the program accounted for only a small part of their total budgets. That point could have been made stronger by showing film clips of hungry children being fed with food donated by American

31

churches, or some similar activity, but ten years ago the courts ruled that it was not a violation of the fairness doctrine for a television program to focus only on the evil that someone might be doing and not even mentioning the good. CBS rose above that dubious standard.

The charges of inaccuracy have been detailed in a letter sent to CBS by attorneys for five of the NCC member churches. The churches should have done their homework better, because their charges of inaccuracy turn out to be quite badly flawed.

CBS charged that in 1981 a "Conference in Solidarity with the Liberation Struggles of Southern Africa" was organized by the United Methodist Church in New York City but ended up being run by the Communist Party and manipulated by the Soviet Union, according to the FBI. The churches deny both charges, saying the conference was organized by the Riverside Church, which is Episcopalian, not the Methodists. However, Methodist headquarters in New York has admitted that they provided both staff and office space to help organize the conference plus a $5000 cash grant which was funneled through the National Council of Churches. The FBI does contend that the conference was actually run by the Communists. That was revealed in a report of the House Intelligence Committee released last December. It is true that some prominent non-communists were listed among the sponsors, as the churches now point out, that in no way rebuts the FBI judgment that the Communists were the prime movers.

The churches also deny that the Washington Office on Latin America, which is supported by the NCC, the WCC, the United Methodists and other churches, distributed a forged document that purported to be an official State Department document on El Salvador. CBS had pointed out that the same forgery had been distributed by the KGB abroad, according to the FBI. This denial is simply not true. A number of people obtained copies of this document from the Washington Office on Latin America.

"60 Minutes" had discussed pro-Castro propaganda material published and distributed by the Cuba Resource Center in New York, which was described as having received heavy support from "National Council member churches." The churches point out that their support of this outfit ended in 1979. They say that no *North American* church has supported it since that time. The Cuba Resource Center continues in operation, but I have been unable to reach them to determine where their support now comes from. It may be from churches that are not in North America. I would agree that CBS should have made it clear that our churches' support of this activity terminated three years ago, but they were justified in using it to show what has been going on.

The churches contend that CBS was wrong in criticizing the NCC and WCC for having given aid to the so-called "new economic zones" in Vietnam. CBS had characterized these as the equivalent of forced labor camps. The churches say that these are areas where volunteers go and are given farms to develop. That isn't the way I heard it. These are areas to which city dwellers have been exiled and forced to try to survive under very difficult conditions. It is a cruel joke to suggest that they are like our homesteaders.

February 18, 1983

8

Who Are The Media Manipulators?

As I travel around the country speaking to a variety of audiences, one question keeps coming up. I am constantly being asked to explain why it is that Big Media so consistently tilt to the liberal-left side of the spectrum. Many of the questioners are convinced that this is the result of the control over the media exercised by a few individuals at the top.

I don't agree with that. My explanation, based on long experience as a media critic, is that the tilt to the left that so many people perceive is a result of the attitudes and beliefs of the reporters, editors, and the producers of TV news programs. For the most part, these important cogs in the media machinery are doing what comes naturally to them, not blindly obeying the orders of their publishers or some shadowy manipulators on the outside.

This has been demonstrated by the very valuable surveys done by Robert Lichter and Stanley Rothman, two scholars who have published a series of articles that probe the attitudes and beliefs of influential figures in the media. In 1981 they gave us a profile of what they called the "media elite." These were 240 writers, editors and executives in the nation's most influential media organizations. This dramatically confirmed the predominance of liberal-left views on the staffs of the big eastern newspapers, news magazines, wire services and TV networks.

In the December-January 1983 issue of the journal, *Public Opinion,* Professors Lichter and Rothman together with Mrs. Linda Lichter have published the results of a similar survey of 104 individuals who play an important role in determining the kind of programs that you see on prime-time television. They describe these as "the cream of television's creative community."

It turns out that the attitudes and beliefs of TV's "creative cream" are remarkably similar to the news media's "elite."

For example, the survey revealed that 82 percent of the TV "cream" had voted for George McGovern over Richard Nixon in 1972. That compares with 81 percent of the media elite who voted for the most radical major party candidate for president in history. How far out of sync they are with the public is shown by the fact that Nixon won a landslide victory, garnering 62 percent of the popular vote.

Things were not much different in 1980. Only 20 percent of the TV "cream" voted for Ronald Reagan. The rest divided their votes among Carter, Anderson and Commoner.

Over two-thirds of both the news media and TV entertainment elites agreed that the government should be redistributing income, and nearly one-third felt that private enterprise is unfair to workers. That didn't mean that they believed in socialism as the solution to all our ills, however. Only 13 percent of the media elite and 19 percent of the TV "cream" believed that big corporations should be publicly owned and operated. Still, I don't find much comfort in learning that one in five of those geniuses who are responsible for our TV entertainment want to see General Motors run like the U.S. Postal Service.

On some of the burning social issues of the day, the near unanimity of the elites is impressive. The TV "cream" favored the pro-choice side of the abortion debate by 97 percent to only 3 percent that took the pro-life side. The media elite were almost as overwhelmingly pro-choice, only 10 percent favoring the pro-life view. Eighty percent of the TV "cream" thought that there is nothing wrong with homosexuality, and 85 percent favored letting homosexuals teach in public schools. The media elite agreed with those positions by 75 percent and 85 percent respectively.

Surprisingly, a very substantial minority of both groups took the view that adultery is wrong. Those who saw nothing wrong with adultery constituted 54 percent of the media elite and 51 percent of the TV "cream."

Two-thirds of those responsible for our TV entertainment fare think television should promote social reform. The reform they favor is making us over in their image.

February 25, 1983

9

Scandal Endangers "60 Minutes"

Next week a judge in Los Angeles may open up the closet door that will expose for all the world to see some very embarrassing skeletons. Judge Bruce Geerneart will be asked to expose to public view films and tapes that show just how CBS produces its popular program, "60 Minutes." An attorney who has seen those films and tapes, Bruce Friedman, says that those supposedly spontaneous, unrehearsed interviews that you see on "60 Minutes" are not that at all.

Quoted in the latest issue of the *AIM Report,* Mr. Friedman says: "These interviews are staged, rehearsed and contrived. The witnesses are in some cases told what to say. There are agreements in advance as to what witnesses are to say, even to the point of concocting a change in the interviewee's story in the middle of the interview."

Friedman has not been at liberty to cite examples to prove his point, because the court ordered CBS to make those films and tapes available to Friedman on the condition that he not reveal their contents. Friedman says that he is shocked by what he has discovered. He says that this could be as big a scandal as the revelation several years ago that participants on the "$64,000 Question" quiz show were being rehearsed.

If what Friedman says is true, it should be a big scandal. The CBS News production standards say: "Broadcasts must be just what they purport to be. We report facts *exactly* as they occur. We do *not* create or change them. It is of the utmost importance, therefore, that these basic principles be adhered to scrupulously by all CBS News Division personnel." An interview is a news event, and the CBS production standards are very explicit about how they should be handled. They say: "Interviews which are not spontaneous and unrehearsed are prohibited unless specifically approved by the president of CBS News. The president will give such approval only in those infrequent and unusual situations where the news importance of the interview clearly outweighs the disadvantages of the procedure and there are sound reasons for the procedure. The extent to which an interview is not spontaneous and unrehearsed must be adequately disclosed in the broadcast."

When did you ever see a "60 Minutes" program carry an announcement informing the viewers that the interviews were not spontaneous and unrehearsed?

Judge Geerneart ordered CBS to let Mr. Friedman have the films and tapes of all the interviews filmed by CBS in connections with a "60 Minutes" program that is now the subject of a libel suit. Friedman is the attorney for the plaintiff in the suit, Dr. Carl A. Galloway, M.D., who claims that he was defamed in a program aired in December 1979 about insurance fraud. Dr. Galloway was described in the program as having signed a fake medical report, a felony in California. He says his signature was forged and that the use of his name was unauthorized. He is suing CBS for $20 million. CBS offered to settle the case out of court for $500,000, his attorney claims, but CBS has denied that offer. The case was scheduled to go to trial February 22, but CBS changed attorneys at the last minute and obtained a two-month delay.

Bruce Friedman doesn't think the public should have to wait another two months to hear what he has discovered on those CBS films and tapes. He says the evidence that "60 Minutes" is not what it purports to be should be disclosed right now, and he is asking Judge Geerneart to vacate the order that he not reveal the contents of the films.

We can't predict which way the judge will rule, but a clue is provided by the comments that he made when he ordered the films to be turned over to Friedman. The judge had examined the transcripts of the interviews and the sound tapes. He noted that the interviews were conducted in a peculiar manner. He said that the questions were first stated "in a leading fashion, even suggesting words that the interviewee might want to use." They were then asked again "without the leading inference, clearly to leave the impression that those words and the momentum of the interview were coming from the interviewee rather than from the interviewer." He thought maybe there should be a program on the way "60 Minutes" is produced. That might be possible if he grants Bruce Friedman's motion to make the films and tapes public.

March 4, 1983

● 10

The Flap Over Canadian Propaganda Films

Relations between the United States and Canada are somewhat strained these days, and at the end of February they were given another jolt as a result of some sloppy reporting by the *Washington Post*. The *Post* stirred up a storm on February 25 by running on page one a story headlined, "U.S. Labels Three Films Propaganda." The films, two about acid rain and the third about nuclear war, had been produced or distributed by the National Film Board of Canada, an agency of the Canadian government.

The films were clearly designed to influence public opinion on controversial political issues. The Canadian Film Board has been registered with the Department of Justice as a foreign agent since 1947. The attorneys for the Justice Department last year made a routine determination that the three films in question were propaganda as defined by the Foreign Agents Registration Act. The Justice Department instructed the Film Board that it would have to attach a notice to each copy of the films stating that it was produced or distributed by a registered foreign agent, whose reports were on file with the Justice Department. Those reports were to include the names of TV stations, theaters or organizations that had used the films, dates of showings and estimated attendance.

The law under which this action was taken has been on the books since 1938, when it was passed to combat the deception of the public by Nazi propaganda. It applies to printed material as well as films. The *Washington Post* has carried many an ad bearing the notification to the readers that the ad was placed by a registered foreign agent. If it has ever objected to that requirement previously it escaped my attention.

Perhaps the *Post* reporter, Cass Peterson, was unaware of all this. She didn't bother to tell her readers about it. She said nothing about when the law was passed, what its purpose is, or the frequency with which it has been enforced. Ms. Peterson quoted Justice Department spokesman John Russell as saying that he had been told that the action was not unique but that he had never heard of its being done before. Mr. Russell says that he knew that the registration statement was regularly required for printed material, but he had not been certain of its application to films. Had Ms. Peterson been a little more thorough, a phone call to the office in charge of foreign agent registration would have made it clear that there was nothing new about the Canadian case.

Unfortunately the *Post* was more interested in getting reactions to a presumed extraordinary act bordering on censorship than in getting the facts about the law and its administration. It devoted 3 paragraphs of its 19-paragraph story to the incomplete information provided by the Justice Department spokesman. Most of the article was devoted to discussing the reactions of Canada's Environment Minister, John Roberts, the National Clean Air Coalition, Dr. Helen Caldicott, the anti-nuclear activist who is the subject of one of the films, the National Film Board of Canada, and Mitch Block, the distributor of the films.

Ms. Peterson used phrases such as "throwback to the McCarthy era," "extraordinary interference with freedom of speech," and "something you would expect from the Soviet Union"—all attributed to named and unnamed Canadians reportedly upset by the U.S. action. In her follow-up story the next day, she reported that "a storm of protest boiled up on Capitol Hill," that the ACLU was planning a court challenge, and that the Canadian embassy had sought clarification and, if possible, reversal of the Justice Department action.

The "storm" was largely stirred up by the inaccurate and irresponsible reporting by the *Post*. In her second story, Ms. Peterson reported that there was nothing unique about the Canadian case and that this same treatment had been given to about 25 foreign films a year for years. But *The Post* didn't apologize. Instead, it ran an editorial that labeled the Justice Department action in enforcing the law "unfortunate." What is unfortunate is the persistence of the *Post* in trying to create scandals where none exist.

March 11, 1983

11

Big Name TV Journalists Expose Themselves

Dan Rather, the anchorman on the CBS Evening News, Tom Brokaw, the co-anchor on the NBC Nightly News, and Sam Donaldson, ABC's White House correspondent who is also a regular on "This Week with David Brinkley," have all given interviews recently to print journalists. The interviews provide colorful confirmation of the charge that the "media elite" are on the liberal-left side of the political spectrum.

Tom Brokaw, who is said to earn about $1 million a year from NBC, gave his interview to *Mother Jones,* a leftwing monthly magazine. He was very hard on Ronald Reagan, describing him as holding values that are "pretty simplistic, pretty old-fashioned," which don't "have much application to what's currently wrong or troubling a lot of people." "Nor do I think he really understands the enormous difficulty a lot of people have in just getting through life, because he's lived in this fantasy land for so long," Brokaw said.

Brokaw explained, "I've always felt one line we've let him get away with is the crock that he was out of work in the '30s, his line that 'I know what it's like.' '' Brokaw said that Ronald Reagan wasn't out of work very long, if he was at all. "He had no real exposure to the rough spots in life," he insisted.

The NBC anchorman said that he had thought from the outset that Reagan's economic theories were a disaster. When the questioner said: "You just criticized members of the business community for keeping their mouths shut even though they knew Reagan's ideas were idiotic," Brokaw responded: "Right."

On El Salvador, Brokaw said that he personally thought it was "outrageous" for the State Department to say that things are getting better and that the country is moving on the road to democracy. He said that his job was to "point out why they're wrong, not become histrionic about it." So much for objective reporting on the NBC Nightly News.

Dan Rather gave his interview to the *Los Angeles Herald-Examiner*. He praised two documentaries that have been shown to be badly flawed—"People Like Us" narrated by Bill Moyers and "The Uncounted Enemy: A Vietnam Deception," which generated a $120 million dollar libel suit filed by General William Westmoreland. Rather said he was very proud of both programs and that he considered the documentary charging Westmoreland with conspiracy to falsify intelligence figures "first rate."

Asked why there were no conservative commentators on network news programs, Rather said: "I don't think the label "liberal-conservative" means very much anymore. There's a danger in that catch phrase. Bill Moyers is by my standards a conservative person. He's not a radical person. A lot of it depends on the prism of your own prejudices. It's how you see them personally. In some corners, Moyer is perceived to be 'liberal.' But if you read Moyer's commentary, I don't think any objective person could do so and come away saying it's a liberal point of view."

Another admirer of Bill Moyer's commentaries is the leftwing magazine, *Mother Jones*. In its May 1982 issue, this magazine praised Moyer's commentaries, saying they displayed a "sense of outrage." They loved it when he "ripped to shreds the logic of the military arms buildup." They were delighted that he had suggested a connection between the assassination of Martin Luther King, Jr. and King's "growing opposition to the Vietnam War." They relished his description of the United States as a society "dependent upon a servant class (where) it is dangerous to demand not only respect for equality, but action to achieve it."

If Bill Moyers looks conservative to Dan Rather, what does that make Rather?

Sam Donaldson's interview in *Playboy* magazine revealed ABC's White House correspondent declaring that he was once a conservative Republican. He said that his politics changed when he came east from his native Texas and began reading the *New York Times* and the *Washington Post*. The interviewer, Peter Manso, said he quickly saw Donaldson's "left-of-center bias," but unlike Brokaw, Sam was careful not to let it all hang out.

March 18, 1983

◉ 12

Journalistic Ethics Illuminated by Filming of Man Afire

A mild furor has arisen over the action of two TV reporters who filmed a man setting himself on fire in Jacksonville, Alabama recently. The TV crew from WHMA-TV in Anniston, Alabama had set up a rendezvous late at night with a caller who said that he was going to burn himself to death to protest against unemployment in America. They notified the police, who scoured the area where the deed was to be done at the appointed hour of 10 P.M., but could find neither the would-be suicide nor the TV crew. They both showed up an hour later, after the police had left the scene.

The man doused himself with lighter fluid. The cameraman focused his camera by zeroing in on the can. The man proceeded to ignite a match, while the camera rolled. The match went out. He lit another, cupping it to protect the flame as he applied the match to his pants. The camera rolled as the pants caught fire and the man tried to beat them out with his hands. He then began to run away, engulfed in flames as the camera continued to record the event. The camera rolled for one minute and 22 seconds, while the two journalists carried out their task of getting a dramatic story. The victim was saved by a volunteer fireman who, attracted by the activity, put out the fire with an extinguisher.

While some of the comment, such as that of Richard Salant, the former president of CBS News and vice chairman of NBC, had been wishy-washy, the conduct of the TV reporters has been the target of some vigorous criticism. The consensus seems to be that they should have behaved as human beings and stopped the man from setting himself on fire.

Agreed. But the conduct of these two young men is more or less in line with new codes of journalistic conduct that have been enunciated by prominent figures in the profession in recent years. Indeed, they might even have been inspired by the famous photo taken in Saigon by an American journalist showing a Buddhist monk immolating himself.

Over the past several years some journalists have been working hard to place their profession not only above the law, but also above morality. They say that they will assume no responsibility for their actions. Indeed, some go so far as to say that it would be a violation of journalistic standards for them to even give thought to the consequences of anything they might do as journalists.

For example, last November *Newsweek* ran an article about how the media deal with national secrets. Noting that some editors said they would not print a story about a CIA covert action if they felt it was necessary, prudent and moral, *Newsweek* said, "The press has no business making such value judgments. Its role in an open society is to print the news, fully and fairly, not to calculate the incalculable consequences..."

Howard Simons, managing editor of the *Washington Post,* said much the same thing at a symposium on national security and freedom of the press last January. He said it was the government's job to keep its secrets. "My job is to find them," he said. Finding them, he would then be inclined to publish them, he said, "because we're not in the business of drawing the moral values."

Lyle Denniston, who covers the Supreme Court for the *Baltimore Sun,* shocked even some of his colleagues with his moral attitude. Asked if he would steal secret documents, Denniston said he would. "Right off Mr. Schlesinger's desk?" he was asked. "Exactly," replied Denniston, "and hopefully without his knowing it."

"Would you hold a gun to his head?" asked Columbia University law professor Benno Schmidt. Denniston replied, "Mayhem might well be ruled out, but I'm not even sure of that."

"But breaking and entering?" asked Schmidt.

"Breaking and entering is benign," replied Denniston. "No problem whatever."

Denniston said, "It's a question of justifying it in terms of the commercial sale of information to interested customers... That's the only thing I do...sell information, hopefully for a profit." It's a short hop from there to filming a suicide for television.

March 25, 1983

13

Media Muffing Pope's Story

In December 1982, CBS News anchorman Dan Rather said that the Bulgarian involvement in the attempted assassination of the Pope was "arguably the story of the decade" if it were true. On March 23, the *New York Times* published a front-page story about important new evidence tying the Bulgarian secret service and the Soviet KGB to the plot to murder the Pope. Unless you are a reader of the *New York Times,* you probably haven't heard about this. Incredible as it may seem even Dan Rather ignored this important confirmation of the truth of what he had called "the story of the decade" three months earlier.

Nicholas Gage of the *New York Times* revealed that an important Bulgarian who defected in France, Iordan Mantarov, has informed French intelligence that the plot to kill the Pope was devised by the Soviet KGB and the Bulgarian secret service. Mantarov told his French debriefers that he was a close friend of a high-ranking official of the Bulgarian state security agency, Dimiter Savov. The French were able to confirm independently that Savov was with the Bulgarian security agency.

Mantarov said his friend had told him that the KGB had become deeply concerned about the growing unrest in Poland in 1979, and they associated it with the election of a Pole, Karol Wojtyla, as Pope. They suspected that this had been engineered by White House national security adviser, Zbigniew Brzezinski, with the idea of using the Catholic Church to destabilize Eastern Europe. Mantarov said that as the unrest mounted in Poland, the KGB began discussions with the Bulgarian secret service on the plot to eliminate the Polish Pope.

Savov had told him, he said, that the Turkish terrorist, Mehmet Ali Agca, had been chosen as the hit man because he was known as a rightist, having killed a liberal Turkish editor in 1979. Agca was spirited out of prison in Turkey under mysterious circumstances. He fled to Bulgaria, where he was equipped with the forged passport that he used on his journey that ended at St. Peter's Square on May 13, 1981. Mantarov said that Agca was supposed to have been killed after he shot the Pope, but that part of the plot was not carried out. Agca, now in prison in Italy, had talked, putting the finger on the Bulgarian agents who had promised to pay him about $1.4 million for the murder.

While Mantarov's story is based on what he says was told to him by his friend, Savov, French intelligence agents believe him because other information that he has attributed to Savov has proven to be accurate. Mantarov defected in France in the summer of 1981, and he presumably gave his information about the Bulgarian connection to the plot to kill the Pope at that time, long before Agca began to talk. The French kept his defection quiet, informing the CIA about it only recently, the *Times* says.

In addition to Mantarov's startling revelations, the *Times* also came up with new facts that buttress the charges against Serge Antonov, the one Bulgarian agent the Italian authorities were able to arrest after Agca talked.

The truth of the Bulgarian and Soviet connection to the plot to kill the Pope is becoming ever more evident. The Soviets have good cause to be worried, because these revelations are destroying the usefulness of their new dictator, Yuri Andropov. It is quite possible that the revelation that Andropov is suffering from both kidney and heart disease on the very day the *New York Times* carried this important story is the beginning of the end for Mr. Andropov. His retirement for reasons of health would spare the Soviets the embarrassment of having their top leader exposed as the man who ordered the Pope's assassination. His death would be even more convenient.

It is shocking that so few of our major papers have reported these discoveries of the *Times*. The *Washington Post* has ignored them, giving the excuse that they can't quote the *New York Times*. That would be embarrassing, an admission that they had been scooped. A half dozen other papers I examined apparently felt the same way. Even Dan Rather ignored this development in what he had called the most important story of the decade.

April 1, 1983

◉ 14

Some Media Cover Up For KGB

On March 24, 1983, Congressman Bill Young of Florida put in the Congressional Record an FBI report titled "Soviet Active Measures Relating to the U.S. Peace Movement." The report began as follows:

"Soviet leaders have publicly backed the peace and nuclear freeze movements, seeing an opportunity to encourage opposition in the West to current U.S. arms control and defense policies. Through official communiques, propaganda, and active measures operations (covert actions), the Soviets have maneuvered to align themselves with popular sentiments of the peace movements in the United States and Western Europe, with the prospect that Western public opinion might dissuade Western governments from deploying the new weapons systems.

"The Soviet organizations principally involved in the Soviet peace offensive in the United States are the KGB and the International Department of the Central Committee, Communist Party of the Soviet Union. The principal objectives of the KGB are to collect information on the U.S. peace movement and to recruit sources to penetrate and influence the movement.

"The CPSU International Department directs the activities of the principal instruments of the Soviet campaign to penetrate and influence the U.S. peace movement, Soviet controlled international front organizations and their U.S. affiliates, the Communist Party, U.S.A. and its front organizations, and the National Council of American-Soviet Friendship."

The FBI report identifies a half dozen Soviet-front groups active in the peace and nuclear freeze movements in this country. It says: "KGB officers have also collected personal and biographical information on several peace activists in the United States. The purpose of this exercise is to identify those peace activists who are likely to cooperate with the Soviet government and to determine if any of these individuals are vulnerable to Soviet recruitment operations."

Discussing the huge anti-nuclear rally staged in New York City's Central Park on June 12, 1982, the FBI says: "Soviet-controlled organizations participated at the highest levels of the June 12 Committee and exerted pressure on the June 12 Committee to focus on U.S. nuclear weapons policies as opposed to Soviet policies." The FBI adds, "Of course the Soviets exploited this large demonstration in its worldwide propaganda campaign against new American weapons."

This report, which was released after still classified information had been deleted, discussed in some detail the roles played by the KGB and the Soviet-front groups which operate freely in this country. It is an eye-opener for those who have read it. It should have been a major news story, but most of our media didn't see it that way.

The *New York Times* put the story on page one under the headline: "F.B.I. Rules Out Russian Control of Freeze Drive." The *Washington Post* headline on page 7 read: "Soviet Role in Nuclear Freeze Limited, FBI Says." Roger Mudd on NBC said the report "runs counter to President Reagan's claim that the nuclear freeze movement is being manipulated by the Soviet Union." CBS and NBC television news ignored the story, but Stephanie Shelton on CBS Radio said the report "contradicts the President's insinuations about the nuclear freeze movement, the report saying that the Soviet Union does not directly control or manipulate it."

All implied or said that President Reagan was wrong in saying at a news conference last November that there was evidence of foreign involvement in the freeze campaign. He had said there was no question but that "foreign agents were sent to help instigate and help create and keep such a movement going." Reagan didn't say that the Soviets *controlled* the movement.

The FBI report *confirms* the active involvement of Soviet agents. It says the Soviets don't view direct control as necessary to achieve their goals. The media were so anxious to prove Reagan wrong that they failed to tell what the FBI was really saying.

April 8, 1983

◉ 15

Leftist Think Tank's Media Ties Exposed

The weekly conservative paper, *Human Events*, has just published a dynamite expose of the close ties that exist between the far-left think tank, the Institute for Policy Studies, and a number of important journalists. The article names prominent journalists who have lectured at the IPS "Washington School." These lecturers include the foreign editor of the *Washington Post*, Karen DeYoung, who was paid $1,000 by the IPS for teaching a course.

Miss DeYoung covered Central America for the *Washington Post* during the successful struggle by the communist-led Sandinistas to overthrow Anastasio Somoza in Nicaragua. Her reporting of that conflict has been criticized by Pulitzer-prize winning correspondent Shirley Christian of the *Miami Herald*, who observed that Miss DeYoung had failed to alert her readers to the fact that the Sandinista leadership was under the control of hardline communists.

Cliff Kincaid, the author of the *Human Events* expose of the IPS-Media axis, reveals that Miss DeYoung is not very skilled at spotting the Marxist ideology. She told Kincaid that the Institute for Policy Studies "doesn't stand for an ideology." Perhaps she thinks that the fact that it always comes out on the left side of political issues is just an accident. Kincaid notes that after visiting a Sandinista training camp during the Nicaraguan civil war, DeYoung wrote an article disputing Somoza's claim that the Sandinistas were communist terrorists. She reported the Sandinista claim that they were committed to the establishment of a "pluralistic democracy," not a "new Cuba."

Miss DeYoung told her IPS class that "most journalists now, most Western journalists at least, are very eager to seek out guerrilla groups, leftist groups, because you assume they must be the good guys."

Kincaid reports that Miss DeYoung invited another *Washington Post* editor, Peter Osnos, to lecture to her class. Even though Osnos had served as the *Post's* correspondent in Moscow, he told the class that he was ignorant of the ultimate intentions and goals of the Soviet Union. Osnos said: "I've given up trying to decide why they do what they do because they're aggressive or because they're scared." Writing from Cuba in 1979, Osnos reported that "the Kremlin is not in charge here." Just how he divined that Castro can thumb his nose at the Soviet Union, which props up Cuba's floundering economy with $3 billion in aid each year, no one knows.

Other prominent journalists who have taught or lectured for the IPS, according to IPS literature, include the president of National Public Radio (NPR), Frank Mankiewicz. NPR's news programs, "All Things Considered" and "Morning Edition" are far enough to the left to delight the IPS. Mr. Mankiewicz, a keen political operative who helped manage George McGovern's campaign for the presidency in 1972, told Kincaid that he didn't remember if he got paid for teaching at the IPS. He also disclaimed knowledge of where the IPS stood on the political spectrum, saying, "I really don't know the institutional position of the IPS. I'm not even sure they've put out documents on behalf of their position . . ."

Indeed they have put out many documents on behalf of their position. In 1978, they put out one that proposed cutting the U.S. defense budget by 50 percent, withdrawing from

NATO and disengaging in the Middle East. It also proposed that the federal government purchase majority ownership of at least one leading firm in each major growth center of the economy.

Kincaid shows that the IPS has been successful in getting its people on network television programs. IPS boasts that commentaries by its fellows are heard regularly over Frank Mankiewicz's tax-payer funded National Public Radio. Articles by its people appear frequently in major newspapers such as the *New York Times*. Kincaid says these liberal media never identify IPS or its fellows as radicals, leftists or Marxists.

Kincaid's article is an invaluable expose of how the IPS has won friends and influenced our media.

April 15, 1983

● 16

Secretary Watt Gets a Bum Rap

The country was "rocked" last week by stories blasting Secretary of the Interior James Watt for what some seemed to think was a grievous crime—his decision not to have a rock band play at the Fourth of July celebration in Washington, D.C. this year. As the story made its way around the country, set off by an interview Secretary Watt gave to the *Washington Post,* Mr. Watt had banned rock music from the Mall where the annual Fourth of July festivities are held in the nation's capital. What was worse, from some of the press accounts, Watt had specifically banned the Beach Boys, a soft rock band whose respectability was attested to by Vice President Bush and First Lady Nancy Reagan.

Mr. Watt was ridiculed by talk show hosts, columnists and editorial writers for this alleged "gaffe." The White House itself succumbed to the stream of media abuse of the Secretary, and the President presented him with a cast of a foot with a hole in it, suggesting that Mr. Watt had shot himself in the foot. Watt got a very bum rap, and the media totally missed and misrepresented what lay behind the action he took with respect to the Fourth of July program.

First of all, Secretary Watt never mentioned the Beach Boys or any other rock group. He told the *Washington Post* reporter that the program this year would be "patriotic, family-based entertainment" featuring the Army Blues Band and Wayne Newton, a singer who has the most successful long-running show in Las Vegas. Last year the program featured a rock group called "the Grass Roots," and Mr. Watt said he had decided to get away from rock music because it had attracted "the wrong element." He had in mind the drug users and heavy drinkers. There had been a lot of those at the concert in 1982. In fact, 52 persons were arrested on charges of drunkenness, drug use and disorderly conduct.

Andrew Baroch, a reporter who covered the event for the Associated Press, said that his strongest impression after the event was the terrible mess that was left on the Mall. The National Park Service estimated that it cost the taxpayers $30,000 to clean it up and haul away the 45 truck-loads of garbage left behind. A Park Service spokesman said the worst problem was the broken glass. It took several days to get that cleaned up.

The Park Service was unhappy about all that. In addition, the District of Columbia Congress of Parent-Teacher Associations and the National Federation for Drug Free Youth were very unhappy about the heavy use of drugs and the unwholesome environment. Mr. William Brown of the Congress of P-TA's said that he was critical of Secretary Watt for not having acted a lot sooner to halt this. He said that he had tried to warn the authorities what was going to happen before July 4th last year. Mr. Brown said that the character of the festivities had changed in recent years, and that he did not want to take his children to the Mall to celebrate the Fourth as he used to do. The main problem was the drug use and the drinking, and he agreed that the rock music tended to attract people who did those things.

Mr. Brown was particularly upset about the "smoke-in" sponsored by an organization that favors legalization of marijuana. This had been staged in Lafayette Park in front of the White House for several years. With the advent of the rock concerts on the Mall, the drug pushers have had a larger receptive crowd to work on. The PTA s have obtained a permit to use Lafayette Park on July 4, 1983 for a family-type program, infuriating the pro-drug group.

Carolyn Burns of the National Federation for Drug Free Youth says the media treated Watt's action "shamefully." She says rock concerts everywhere serve as "safehouses" for drug users, and the concerts on the Mall were no exception. The media reported the views of the pro-drug and pro-rock people, but they never interviewed Brown or Burns. Nor did they report that Mr. Watt had simply ratified a recommendation of the Park Service.

April 22, 1983

17

A Bad Day at Black Rock

No one jumped off the roof of "Black Rock," the New York skyscraper that CBS calls home, but April 21, 1983 was a bad day at Black Rock. First, Judge Pierre N. Leval ruled that CBS would have to hand over the Benjamin report to Gen. William C. Westmoreland and his attorneys. The Benjamin report is a 61-page summation of the investigation CBS made into charges that its employees had violated company guidelines in making the documentary that inspired Gen. Westmoreland's $120 million libel suit against CBS. The documentary, which was titled "The Uncounted Enemy: A Vietnam Deception," had alleged that Westmoreland had conspired to understate the strength of the enemy forces in Vietnam with disastrous results.

CBS had one of its executives investigate charges that the procedures had rigged the documentary to "convict" Gen. Westmoreland and had violated CBS News rules against rehearsing witnesses, paying witnesses, and other unethical practices in the process. When the much-publicized investigation was completed, CBS promptly declared the findings to be secret. That gave rise to strong suspicions that the investigation had confirmed the charges of wrongdoing, although CBS denied that.

The excuse CBS gave for its secrecy was that the employees who had been interviewed about the charges of wrongdoing had been promised confidentiality. They argued that this was necessary for them to conduct in-house reviews of their performance. ABC, NBC, *Newsweek,* and Dow-Jones all told the judge that they agreed with CBS on this point, but most of the media were silent. They didn't put any pressure on CBS to release the report, but they couldn't bring themselves to argue that the full disclosure that they tend to demand of everyone else should not apply to CBS.

CBS has asked for a stay of the judge's ruling, and they will try to get it reversed. Their tenacious fight to keep the Benjamin report secret suggests they have a lot to hide. That was made apparent on the night of April 21, when Hodding Carter III dissected the CBS documentary on Gen. Westmoreland on his PBS program, "Inside Story."

Hodding Carter, the State Department spokesman during the Carter Administration, had originally been impressed by the CBS charges against Westmoreland. He had written an article for the *Wall Street Journal* praising the program. After looking into the matter more carefully, he has changed his mind. His PBS program devastated CBS.

The CBS documentary had been faulted from the very beginning for not having included interviews with several important people who would have given evidence that contradicted what CBS was trying to prove. One of these was Lt. Gen. Phillip Davidson, who was Gen. Westmoreland's top intelligence officer at the time the conspiracy was alleged to have taken place. Davidson had never been interviewed by CBS, although, as he told Hodding Carter, he would have had to have been at the center of any conspiracy to alter intelligence data had such a conspiracy existed.

George Crile, the producer of the CBS program, said that he had not interviewed Davidson because he understood that he was very ill. Gen. Davidson told Hodding Carter that during the period the documentary was being made he had remarried and had been playing golf almost daily. He said CBS had never contacted him.

Hodding Carter showed George Crile asking, "What is it that Davidson has to say that we should have included in there?" He then shows Davidson saying, "Neither Gen. Westmoreland nor anyone else in a position of authority over me ever gave me any order, any directive, any hint, any indication to manipulate and distort figures, to minimize enemy strength figures or to suppress them."

The same technique was used to show that CBS had misrepresented or suppressed what had been said by two other important witnesses, Walt Rostow, President Johnson's national security adviser, and Gen. George Godding. Both contradicted statements CBS included in its documentary. True, this has all been said before, but Hodding Carter demonstrated that the best way to answer TV distortion is to expose it on TV.

April 29, 1983

WATCH OUT FOR THE BEE DROPPINGS, COMRADE.

18

Secret Report Devastates CBS

For nine months CBS refused to make public the report of an investigation into charges of serious wrongdoing at CBS News. The investigation was carried out by Burton Benjamin, senior executive/producer at CBS News, after *TV Guide* magazine revealed that documents and information leaked from CBS showed "how CBS broke the rules and 'got' Gen. Westmoreland." *TV Guide* charged that the producers of the controversial documentary that accused Westmoreland of faking intelligence data in Vietnam had violated CBS News guidelines in their effort to prove their case.

The *TV Guide* charges hit CBS like a bombshell. After all, CBS News is supposed to be the recipient of leaks, not a source of them. It promptly announced that Benjamin had been assigned to make a thorough investigation. CBS News President Van Gordon Sauter was quoted as saying, "We will find and then go right to the public to say this is what we found."

It didn't quite work that way. Benjamin's lengthy report was ready by mid-July, but its findings were so damaging that

Mr. Sauter had second thoughts about telling the public what the report said. It was kept completely secret. On July 15, 1982, Mr. Sauter issued a 1300-word memo, which he described as the conclusions reached by himself, Mr. Benjamin and CBS News Vice President Edward Joyce. Demands that the full text of the Benjamin report be made public were rejected.

Nine months later the Benjamin report was pried out of CBS by a court order obtained by Gen. Westmoreland, who is suing the newtwork for libel to the tune of $120 million. The report is devastating to the credibility of CBS News. No wonder they refused to release it voluntarily. Sauter said in his memo, "The greatest asset of CBS News is its credibility. Protecting that credibility is the most important thing we at CBS News do..." CBS tried to protect its credibility by suppressing the Benjamin report. That effort has now backfired.

Here are some of the charges *TV Guide* made which Benjamin found to be true.

1. CBS set out to prove Westmoreland guilty of conspiracy.

2. They selected persons to be interviewed who would support that charge and ignore those who had evidence that refuted it.

3. They paid the chief witness against Westmoreland, Sam Adams, $25,000.

4. When another witness, George Allen, didn't give the answers they wanted, they flagrantly violated CBS rules by showing him tapes of other interviews, and then interviewed him again.

5. They didn't challenge the credibility of Adams and other witnesses used against Westmoreland, giving them "soft" questions.

6. Westmoreland was not adequately informed of the subject he was to be interviewed about, with the result that he was not well prepared to discuss 14-year old statistics. When he misstated a figure which he subsequently corrected by mail, the correction was ignored and the error used to help make the case against him.

7. Westmoreland's repeated assertion in his interview that the Vietcong Tet offensive in January 1968 showed that his esti-

mate of enemy strength were too high, not too low, as CBS charged, was edited out. Gen. Daniel Graham's statement to the same effect was also suppressed, even though Graham had agreed to do the interview on the condition that he be permitted to make this statement. Benjamin failed to discuss the importance of the suppression of this information. It goes to the heart of the CBS charge that Westmoreland had brought about a disaster at Tet because he held down estimates of Vietcong strength for political reasons. Since Tet was a military victory for our side and since the Vietcong forces that took part in the Tet offensive were consistent with Westmoreland's estimates, this information had to be excluded from the CBS documentary to keep it from self-destructing.

The report is a damning document both for what it says and what it carefully avoids.

May 6, 1983

◉ 19

Jack Anderson Spiked
Selectively

Recently the *Washington Post* refused to run (spiked) a column by Jack Anderson which reported that nine present or former members of Congress, including Ted Kennedy, had been implicated in the Capitol Hill drug scandal. Allegations had previously surfaced against four of those named by Anderson—Barry Goldwater, Jr., a former Republican congressman from California, Charles Wilson, a conservative Democrat from Texas, Fred Richmond, a liberal Democrat from New York who is currently serving a term in prison, and Ronald Dellums, a radical Democrat from California.

The allegations against these four had all been reported by the *Washington Post*. Anderson came up with five more names— Ted Kennedy, Gerry Studds, a radical Democrat from Massachusetts, Parren Mitchell, a radical Democrat from Maryland, John Burton, a former Democratic Congressman from California who also was on the far left, and Lionel Van Deerlin, a formal liberal Democratic Congressman from California.

According to Robert McCloskey, ombudsman for the

Washington Post, Ben Bradlee, the paper's executive editor, killed the Anderson column because it "failed any reasonable test of credibility." He thought it would be unfair to the persons named to publish it. Mr. McCloskey agreed with that decision, but he noted that the *Post* had not hesitated to report the charges against Reps. Goldwater and Wilson, which were based on anonymous sources. The paper had given extensive space to allegations that the mayor of Washington, D. C., Marion Barry, had used cocaine, even though its own investigation had concluded that there was no evidence to support the charge. In another story, the *Post* had said that Goldwater, Wilson and Dellums "have been the subject of unsubstantiated allegations."

McCloskey confessed to being troubled by the inconsistency of the editors of the *Post.* His column did nothing to allay the suspicion that Anderson's column was not spiked because it made unsubstantiated allegations. Such allegations are, after all, Jack Anderson's stock in trade. The problem, it seems clear, was not what was said, but who was named, especially Senator Kennedy and his daughter.

In February and March, the *Washington Post* ran five columns by Anderson which reported an allegation that Sen. Strom Thurmond, a conservative Republican from South Carolina, had taken bribes of $20,000 or more. Two columns implied that Sen. Thurmond had used his influence as head of the Senate Judiciary Committee to have the man who was Anderson's source indicted on criminal charges.

These serious charges were run without the slightest indication on the part of the *Washington Post* that it had any doubts about the credibility of Anderson's source. Once the source became known, however, it became obvious that questions should have been raised. The man had briefly worked for Honeywell Corp. He had been discharged in April 1982. Honeywell charged that he had set up a bogus corporation which he used to bill Honeywell for services that had never been rendered. He was also charged with having defrauded the company of relocation expenses and having falsified a deed. Altogether, Anderson's source was indicted on six counts of fraud.

Moreover, others who had dealings with this individual

have said that he has a reputation for telling wild stories and is not to be trusted. He himself raised the claim that he was indicted because of the allegations he had made against Sen. Thurmond, but it seems quite likely that it was the other way around. He may have made the charges against the senator because he knew that he was going to be indicted and he figured that he might gain sympathy and attention by claiming that he was being persecuted by the chairman of the Senate Judiciary Committee.

Anderson, who has trouble finding enough scandals in Washington to keep his daily column interesting, ran with this wild story. The Justice Department investigated and concluded that there was no substantiation whatever for the charges. The *Post* reported that in a few lines. That's a far cry from the protective treatment afforded Sen. Kennedy.

May 13, 1983

◉ 20

Newsweek's Disgraceful Performance

Two years ago we were shocked when it was revealed that the *Washington Post* had been taken in by reporter Janet Cooke's fake story about an eight-year-old heroin addict who did not exist. The *Post* had to return the Pulitzer prize the story had won. The case focused attention on the risks that editors run when they don't insist that reporters tell them who their sources are.

Now the German magazine *Stern*, the *London Times*, the *New York Post* and other papers in the Murdoch chain and *Newsweek* magazine have made the same embarrassing error on even a grander scale. They were taken in by the forged Hitler diaries, which they all publicized massively. *Stern* is said to have paid over $4 million for the fake diaries, even though the management did not know their source. The reporter who made the deal insisted that identities of the sellers had to be kept secret because lives might be endangered. That, incidentally, was the same reason Janet Cooke gave the editors of the *Washington Post* for not telling them the identity of her eight-year-old heroin addict.

The *London Times* had agreed to pay *Stern* $400,000 for the right to publish the Hitler diaries after their expert, historian Hugh Trevor-Roper, had attested to their authenticity. *Newsweek* was on the verge of buying the rights reportedly for $3 million, but they decided against it for two reasons. *Newsweek* wanted "more systematic and authoritative authentication," and they objected to Stern's plan to stretch out publication over 18 months. *Newsweek* Editor Maynard Parker said that *Stern* did not want to run the material about the holocaust until the very end. He said, "That seemed to me to be intolerable from our point of view and irresponsible."

Newsweek didn't declare the diaries to be genuine, but it leaned heavily in that direction. It devoted its cover and 13 pages of the May 2 issue to the story of the diaries. It reported the opinions of experts who thought the diaries were fake, but it gave greater attention to those who suspended judgment or thought they might be genuine. Kenneth Rendell, a "documents expert" hired by *Newsweek* was quoted as saying, "I have no evidence whatsoever to believe that the diaries are fakes, but there's no evidence (so far) to believe that they're genuine." *Newsweek's* editors' leaning was indicated by where they inserted that "so far."

Editor Maynard Parker gave an interview to Hodding Carter, host of the PBS program "Inside Story," in which he said, "It's an extraordinary historic find, and that's why we knew it would be a terrific story. That's why we went with it like we did." That was aired May 4. Within hours the West German government revealed that the diaries were forgeries, a finding that was based both on technical analysis of the paper, bindings and glue in the notebooks used, but also on the fact that the contents were clearly based on a book published in 1962 entitled *Hitler's Speeches and Proclamations—1932-45.*

Newsweek promptly came out with another cover story on the diaries in its May 9 issue. This time the cover title read, "Forgery, Uncovering the Hitler Hoax." The story noted that several reputations had been damaged by the discovery of the fraud. It mentioned the *Stern* management, editors and reporter Gerd Heidemann, Rupert Murdoch the owner of the *London Times* and other papers that had bought the rights to the diaries, and historian Hugh Trevor-Roper, whose authentication of the diaries had led Murdoch to make the purchase. It asked how so many people had been "sucked in so deeply."

Missing from the list of battered reputations was *Newsweek* and its editor, Maynard Parker. Missing was an explanation of how *Newsweek,* which unlike the others had not paid any money for the rights to the diaries, had nevertheless capitalized on them by running that extraordinary cover story, featuring Hitler on the cover. Two of the seven pages were devoted to Kenneth Rendell's new judgment that the diaries "looked wrong" at first glance and were obvious forgeries on closer inspection. *Newsweek* didn't say why it couldn't have waited for Rendell's opinion before running that cover story.

May 20, 1983

⊙ 21

The Silent Treatment for Sakharov

President Reagan proclaimed May 21 "Andrei Sakharov Day," honoring the brilliant Russian physicist and Nobel Peace Prize winner who languishes in internal exile in the Soviet Union. Sakharov, who is known as the father of the Soviet H-bomb, has long been a leader of the human rights movement in the Soviet dictatorship. He was awarded the Nobel Peace Prize for his efforts, but the Soviets responded by sending him off to the city of Gorky in January 1980. Gorky is off-limits to Westerners, and Sakharov is effectively cut off from contact with western reporters, as well as other human rights activists.

In 1981, Sakharov attracted worldwide attention to his treatment by going on a hunger strike that lasted 17 days. Since then he has suffered two heart attacks. In proclaiming Sakharov Day, President Reagan said that Andrei Sakharov's bold and penetrating voice is in danger of being stilled. He said, "Not only is he denied his freedom, but his health is in danger, jeopardized by constant harrassment and lack of decent medical attention."

But it is not only harrassment and his health that is silencing Sakharov. The American media are falling down in their job of keeping the burning issue of the shameful treatment of this great man by the communists a burning issue. The reporting of the proclamation of Sakharov Day by President Reagan is a case in point.

The *New York Times,* which is the newspaper of record in this country, reported the President's action in a 40-word Reuter's dispatch on page A9. The *Washington Post,* the most widely read paper in the nation's capital, covered this story with 65 words from a UPI dispatch that it ran on page A3. The television network evening news shows ignored the story altogether.

Washington's new daily, the *Washington Times,* which just celebrated its first birthday, did a great deal better. It carried a 240-word story by one of its own reporters on page 3. It followed up the next day with a strong editorial which said, "It behooves Americans, so profoundly favored in this vicious world and often so complacent in our rare fortune, to reflect on the continuing ordeal the Soviet Union is visiting upon those of its citizens who are audacious enough to defy totalitarianism. Sakharov is a poignant symbol of the courage such defiance requires—and the crushing callousness with which the communist state responds to such courage."

The *Washington Post* pointed out that President Reagan had said that the treatment of Sakharov demonstrated that the communists "are aware of the shakiness of their rule and the fragility of their claims of legitimacy." He added, "And that is why they seek to stifle dissent." Many in the media howled with outrage when in his recent speech in Orlando, Florida President Reagan described the Soviet Union as the "focus of evil" in the world. But when the President cites as evidence of that evil the treatment of Andrei Sakharov, our big media ignore his words.

This is a great tragedy. Sakharov's wife, Elena Bonner, recently said that if Western interest in her husband diminishes, the secret police "will one day come and kill him." That is one reason why it was important for the President to designate Sakharov Day. But the efforts of the President and Sakharov's family and friends are to some extent negated when the Big Media in this country ignore or downplay this symbolic action.

This heartens the oppressors in the Kremlin, since it suggests to them that the American media don't really care much about Andrei Sakharov.

Sakharov himself is well aware of the great importance of obtaining the cooperation of the Western media in the difficult struggle for freedom in the Soviet Union. He smuggled out a message to the International Sakharov Hearings that were held in Washington in September 1979. In it he expressed the hope that the media should give the hearings the widest possible publicity, exposing the crimes of communism. His hope was disappointed. Our media virtually ignored the hearings, leaving the participants who had come from many countries angry and disgusted. Three months later the Soviets arrested Sakharov.

May 27, 1983

◉ 22

How the *Times* Trashed Teller

Dr. Edward Teller is one of America's national treasures. He doesn't like to be called the father of the H-bomb, but the fact is that it was not only his genius but his persistence that enabled us to beat the Soviets in the development of that weapon. He prevailed over those such as Dr. Robert Oppenheimer who suddenly developed dovish tendencies once the Germans and Japanese were defeated in World War II. Dr. Teller is not only a brilliant scientist, but unlike Oppenheimer he never suffered any illusions about the good intentions of Stalin or his successors. He knows that for freedom to survive, we must have a strong military defense.

Perhaps for that reason, Dr. Teller has not always enjoyed a good press. The media treatment of this distinguished scientist hit a new low on April 28, when the *New York Times* ran a lengthy front-page article by reporter Jeff Gerth which implied that Teller had used his position as a science advisor to the White House to enrich himself. The scenario that emerged from Gerth's article was that Teller had been given a large amount of stock in Helionetics, Inc. because he was known to have influence with the Reagan administration. Gerth reported that Helionetics, a small California high-tech firm, had a laser that could be used as a weapon in space. He reported that Teller had been involved in the preparation of President Reagan's March 23 speech recommending a space-based anti-missile defense system.

Gerth reported that there had been unusual activity in Helionetics stock in the week preceding that speech and that its price had risen sharply. The implication was that Teller had leaked information about the speech to insiders, who had then bought Helionetics stock because the company would benefit greatly from the program that President Reagan proposed. Gerth painted a conflict-of-interest situation, and hinted that Teller might not have disclosed his interest in Helionetics.

The Soviets loved Gerth's story. They immediately picked it up, embellished it a little and broadcast it around the world over Radio Moscow. They used it to prove their favorite propaganda theme that everything that is done in the United States is motivated by personal greed.

Dr. Teller issued a press release refuting the charges in the story. That was generally ignored by the media. I sent the *Times* a letter discussing the errors and false insinuations in the story point by point. The *Times* refused to print it. Not until three weeks after the smear was published did the *Times* run any hint that it might have been incorrect. The paper reported back on page D3 that the White House had cleared Dr. Teller of the charges that he had behaved improperly.

Appalled by the conduct of the *New York Times* and the exploitation of the Gerth story by the Soviets, Accuracy in Media decided to enable Dr. Teller to transmit his rebuttal of the *Times* to the widest possible audience. It purchased a full page in the *Wall Street Journal* of May 31 to publish a statement by Dr. Teller under the headline, "I was NOT the Only Victim of the *New York Times.*"

Dr. Teller pointed out that he had acquired stock in Helionetics by purchase, not as a gift, in 1980, *before* the election of Ronald Reagan. He was impressed by the company's scientists and their ingenious ideas. However, those ideas did not include a weapons-laser, as Gerth had reported. Helionetics' laser can be used for communications but it would be useless against a missile.

Gerth's nasty insinuations are demolished by the facts. Dr. Teller had no knowledge of the content of the President's March 23 speech until two hours before it was delivered. Helionetics did not stand to gain from the proposals made in that speech. The best explanation for the rise in the value of its stock was that it became known that it was going to report record first quarter sales and profits.

Dr. Teller says that Gerth's story diverted attention from testimony he gave that same day supporting Reagan's missile defense proposals. He sees this as one more example of the harm done by the media in publishing "misinformation masquerading as news."

June 3, 1983

⊙ 23

Dan Rather in the Dock

CBS's eight-million-dollar man, Dan Rather, was converted into a Cable News Network star for a few days at the end of May and the beginning of June, and CNN didn't pay Dan a cent. CNN grabbed Dan Rather's services for free by simply televising his testimony in the libel suit that Dr. Carl Galloway brought against CBS, Dan Rather and other CBS employees. In doing so, CNN broke new ground, and it was ground that needed to be broken. They treated the conduct of the news media and journalists as news.

If the trial out in Los Angeles had involved a prominent political figure, say Henry Kissinger, who is almost as well known as Dan Rather, you can rest assured that ABC, CBS and NBC would have been falling over themselves to tell you all about the proceedings on the morning news, the evening news and Nightline. Indeed, note the coverage that the media have given to mere charges made against Dr. Kissinger in a newly published book by journalist Seymour Hersh. NBC's Today Show gave Mr. Hersh an entire half hour to discuss his accusations that Kissinger was duplicitous. ABC's Nightline devoted almost an hour to Hersh and his charge and to rebuttals and comments by Kissinger's former colleagues and two other journalists.

Contrast this with the treatment of the trial of CBS and Dan Rather. The networks have reported it only sporadically. Ironically, the executives at CBS in New York had to watch CNN to see how Rather was doing. There was nothing comparable to 30 minutes on the Today Show or nearly a full hour on ABC's Nightline.

Nightline came close. On May 25, they devoted one segment of the program to a discussion of TV news filming and editing techniques, and they invited me to be one of the guests. The reason for doing the segment was because revelations in the Galloway case had cast grave doubt on the integrity of the popular CBS program, "60 Minutes." It was on "60 Minutes" that Dr. Galloway had been accused of signing a false medical report, a charge that led him to file his $30 million libel suit against CBS. As a result of this suit, a California judge ordered CBS to turn over to Dr. Galloway's attorney the tapes of interviews that had been done for the program but had not been used on the air. These are called "outtakes." After viewing the outtakes, the attorney charged that they revealed a CBS scandal.

For example, one witness had been run through the very same interview three times, each time changing her story halfway through the interview. Another person who was asked how much a cheater would make on a typical fraudulent insurance claim for a car accident went through his answer twice. The second time all his figures were increased by 50 percent, apparently to make them more impressive. This is showbiz, not journalism.

This is the very damaging fallout from the Galloway suit. It has received even less attention from the media than the charges against Dan Rather and his appearance on the witness stand. It is of greater importance for most of us, because it concerns not merely the sloppiness of Dan Rather as a reporter, but the corruption of television journalism by show business.

Although Ted Koppel did not want to discuss the Galloway

case on Nightline, he permitted me to point out on this nationally televised program that CBS had been caught in the act of rehearsing witnesses and apparently advising them what they should say on camera. These are serious violations of CBS News guidelines, which state that all CBS News interviews must be spontaneous and unrehearsed. I suggested that the reluctance of CBS to make its outtakes public was now understandable. They wanted to conceal the fact that they were violating both journalistic ethics and their own guidelines. They wanted confidentiality to conceal their own wrongdoing.

Don Hewitt, the executive producer of "60 Minutes," protested this ABC program the next day, saying that it was unfair to CBS. For once, CBS was on the receiving end of accurate, hard-hitting criticism on national TV. It was overdue.

June 10, 1983

24

Yellow Rain Holds Water

With the *New York Times* taking the lead, some elements of the media at the beginning of June again tried to cast doubt on evidence that the Soviet Union has been using biological warfare in violation of international agreements. On June 1, the *Times* carried a long article by Philip M. Boffey, illustrated with photos, which discussed at length the theory of a Harvard professor that "yellow rain," the toxin that has reportedly caused thousands of deaths in Southeast Asia and Afghanistan, is nothing more than bee excrement.

Prof. Matthew Meselson had reported finding bee pollen in a sample of yellow rain that had been obtained in Thailand by official Canadian observers in February 1982. Another sample collected previously in Laos which had been presented to ABC News also contained pollen according to the professor. Meselson advanced the theory that the highly toxic ingredient in yellow rain, trychothecene mycotoxin, had developed naturally in the accumulated pollen excreted by bees. Ergo, the Soviets were innocent of any wrongdoing.

The *Times* did not point out to its readers that Dr. Meselson has long been searching for reasons to knock down the growing evidence of Soviet use of biological or chemical agents to kill people in Southeast Asia and Afghanistan. The stories of attacks with such weapons began coming out of Laos as early as 1975. Refugees told stories of their villages being attacked with rockets that exploded in the air and released a deadly vapor, usually yellow or white. The refugees said the victims suffered dizziness, severe itching, nausea, shock, bloody diarrhea and vomiting.

The early reports were fragmentary, and no evidence other than refugee accounts was available. But the reports continued and grew in frequency. In 1979 a U.S. army medical team went to Thailand to interview refugees on the subject, and a report of the findings was published. The U.S. government raised the charges that yellow rain was being used with the Soviet Union, Laos and Vietnam. In 1980, similar reports came from Cambodia and also from Afghanistan.

One defector from the Laotian army said that he had been involved in attacking Hmong villages with toxic chemicals. He had been told that the purpose of the attacks was to exterminate the "reactionary Hmong people." Another compilation of eyewitness accounts was published by the State Department in March 1981.

The accounts of victims and eyewitnesses were confirmed by other evidence beginning in 1981. Autopsies were conducted on the victims of a yellow rain attack in Cambodia, and the results pointed to a toxin. Before long, Western experts singled out trichothecene mycotoxins as the agent being used. High levels of these mycotoxins were found on a leaf and stem sample brought out of Cambodia. The level was twenty times greater than any recorded natural outbreak. The State Department noted that only the Soviet Union had the facilities to produce this dangerous poison.

At that time, the *New York Times* took the lead in trying to debunk the evidence presented by the State Department. One of those it quoted then was Prof. Meselson. Subsequently the evidence was strengthened by discovery of a gas mask taken off a dead Soviet soldier in Afghanistan which was contaminated with mycotoxins. Afghan refugees told stories similar to those coming from Laos and Cambodia. Blood samples taken from victims in Cambodia in January 1982 contained a metabolite of T-2 trichothecene toxin.

When Prof. Meselson, a biologist who is known as a "dove" at Harvard came out with his bee excrement theory, journalists who seemed to be eager to let the Soviet Union off the hook rushed to suggest that the U.S. government and all the scientists who had laboriously accumulated the evidence of Soviet perfidy and inhumanity were wrong. Just how the evidence that some pollen was mixed in with a sample of the mycotoxin nullified the evidence of the autopsies, the blood samples, the contaminated gas mask, and the accounts of the victims and the Laotian solider they did not explain.

June 18, 1983

YOUR NEWS MEDIA HASN'T WARNED YOU!

⊙ 25

CBS at Last Enforces Its Rules

A lot of people have been wondering when CBS was going to demonstrate that its vaunted "News Standards" were more than windowdressing. The news standards lay down the law for CBS News correspondents and producers, the guidelines they must follow to insure that what CBS puts on the air is compiled honestly, legally and ethically.

Last July, CBS admitted that there had been some serious violations of those guidelines in the production of the documentary that gave rise to Gen. William C. Westmoreland's $120 million libel suit against CBS. Those violations were revealed more starkly last April when CBS, responding to a court order, coughed up the Benjamin report. That was the report of the investigation that CBS itself had made of charges of wrongdoing in the production of the Westmoreland documentary.

The report showed that producer George Crile had coached and rehearsed witnesses even though the news standards say that interviews must be "spontaneous and unrehearsed" except in unusual circumstances. In those exceptional cases the president of CBS News must give his permission and the audience must be told that the interview is not spontaneous and unrehearsed. There was no permission given for rehearsed interviews for the Westmoreland documentary, nor was the audience told about the rehearsing.

The report also showed that Mr. Crile had paid a $25,000 consultant's fee to Sam Adams, the man who was behind the charge that Gen. Westmoreland had conspired to alter intelligence data on enemy strength in Vietnam. Adams was also one of the persons used in the documentary to make the charges against Gen. Westmoreland. The news standards say that when a paid consultant is interviewed for a broadcast the audience must be informed that the individual is a paid consultant. No such disclosure was made with respect to Sam Adams.

CBS took no disciplinary action against George Crile even though they knew in July 1982 that he had been responsible for very serious violations of CBS News rules. He was even assigned to produce a new documentary. It was nearing completion when suddenly, on June 15, CBS announced that it was suspending Crile, with full pay, however, for a newly discovered violation of the rules.

This violation was the taping of a telephone conversation without telling the other person that the conversation was being tape-recorded. A few years ago, before tape recorders became so common, that was a no-no, but it is a common practice today, and it is not a violation of either federal law or the law in New York, where Mr. Crile has his office. True, it is a violation of the CBS News standards, which require that this not be done without first clearing it with the president of CBS News or his designee in consultation with the Law Department. The reason given is because in some states the practice is still illegal.

In other words, CBS did not see this as an ethical problem. It was strictly a matter of making sure that it was legal. Crile knew that what he was doing was legal, and he didn't bother to check with the CBS lawyers. It is hard to believe that CBS would suspend him for such a petty technical violation when they had for nearly a year done nothing about the far more serious violations of the rules that Mr. Crile had committed.

Perhaps nothing would have happened if the secret taping

had not involved an interview with such a prestigious person as former Defense Secretary Robert McNamara. Mr. McNamara was indignant when he found that his off-the-record interview had been recorded. The whole thing broke into print after Gen. Westmoreland's attorney learned about the McNamara tape and complained about its not having been turned over to him. Attorneys for CBS at first said that it had been lost or destroyed. That, too, was embarrassing.

It seems that Crile's chief offense has been causing CBS embarrassment, not violating their rules. He has been lowered over the side ever so gently, with full pay, perhaps in the hope that he will not blab to the press that he was only doing what many others have been doing at CBS for years. That would be even more embarrassing.

June 24, 1983

26

McCarthyism at ABC News

One of the great myths of the present day is that the 1950s were a period of terror in the United States presided over by the grand inquisitor, Senator Joseph McCarthy. This is an idea that has been spread by the media, and it has been accepted without question by many people who had no personal knowledge of that period. On June 23, ABC News added to the myth by airing an hour-long program titled "McCarthyism: 'The American Inquisition'."

The ads for the program said: "Senator Joe McCarthy claimed he was saving our society from communism. But thousands of ordinary Americans lost their livelihoods and their homes. Without real evidence, without hard proof, without even knowing their accusers. It's thirty years later. And still they suffer. The survivors of a time of fear and suspicion, each still serving the sentence of a disrupted life."

That is a good summary of the myth, but it was a very poor description of the program that ABC aired. ABC served up two cases of persons who had lost their jobs over thirty years ago on the ground that they were security risks. If they were the best cases ABC could find to make the case that there were thousands of innocent victims of McCarthyism, then a good case might be made that their ad for the program was false.

The first case concerned a man named Paul McCarty, who lost his job as an electrical construction worker with the Atomic Energy Commission in 1953 after the agency denied him a security clearance. The AEC had been provided with information by the FBI that indicated that McCarty had communist ties of some kind. McCarty has obtained his FBI files, and he was shown reading them in front of the ABC camera. ABC never told the viewers just what the charges against McCarty were. Nor did they mention that the AEC had given McCarty a hearing, after which it reached the decision that he was a security risk.

That may have been an unjust decision. McCarty insists that it was, but ABC did not even describe the evidence against McCarty, much less produce any proof that the evidence was conclusively false. Nor did they mention that the decision was made by the AEC, not the FBI, which acted solely as the gatherer of raw information in this case. McCarty insists he was wronged, and ABC accepted that as fact. It further gave the impression that McCarty was unable to hold a job in the construction industry for the next thirty years for any length of time because of this blot on his record. There are many jobs in the construction industry that don't require security clearances. It is absurd to blame all of McCarty's subsequent problems on that.

The second case was equally unconvincing. An art teacher, Luella Mundel, was dismissed from her job in the small town of Fairmont, West Virginia. Miss Mundel had views that were clearly not congenial to the inhabitants of Fairmont. She was accused of being an atheist, of having liberal views on sexual matters, and she painted surrealistic pictures. Those were not popular positions in Fairmont in 1951. According to ABC, she was dismissed as a security risk after she stood up at an American Legion Americanism seminar and challenged statements made by the speakers.

One speaker was the journalist and author, Victor Lasky,

who told ABC that he had talked about the nature of communist infiltration, but had warned against witch-hunts. Asked about Luella Mundel, Lasky said that he recalled that a hysterical woman had assailed him and the other speakers. "I had to respond to calm her down," he said.

But ABC got a different version from a resident of Fairmont who was shown saying: "As I recall, Mr. Lasky called her a communist. This seemed to agitate her very much, and she called him a Nazi...." Lasky says that's absurd. He points out that soon after he got a letter from a friend of Miss Mundel's saying that he had impressed her as a compassionate man and asking if he wouldn't help Miss Mundel with her job problem.

ABC had a copy of that letter, but with a reckless disregard of the truth that has come to be called "McCarthyism," they left the impression that Lasky was the cause of Mundel's losing her job. Miss Mundel found another teaching job in a more congenial state. She did not lose her livelihood, and she's not "serving the sentence of a disrupted life."

July 1, 1983

⊙ 27

Leaks the Media Don't Like

Leaks are the mother's milk of the Washington media. They win Pulitzer prizes with them. The reporters and editors swear they will go to jail before divulging the source of a leak. Why? Because divulging a source would discourage further leaks, and without leaks what would an investigative reporter do? How would he win prizes, promotions and national notoriety?

The general rule is that all leaks to journalists serve the national interest even though they may involve the exposure of national security secrets, covert operations, and/or the frustration of important national policies.

There is one exception to that general rule. Leaks from within a news organization to an outside journalist may not serve the national interest. Some journalists think that such leaks are evil and should be condemned. This became evident in May 1982, when *TV Guide* published an article based on leaked documents and information from within CBS News. It revealed that there had been serious violations of CBS News

Standards and journalistic ethics in the production of the documentary that inspired General Westmoreland's $120 million libel suit against CBS. It was a great coup. It forced CBS to make an investigation. The findings fully confirmed the accuracy of the leaked information, but CBS kept the report secret for nearly a year. The media did not demand its release.

The *TV Guide* scoop was received sourly by most of the media. The *Washington Post* and *Newsweek* magazine ran articles about it which devoted more space to attacking *TV Guide* than to reporting what it had discovered about the wrongdoing inside CBS News. Even when the Society of Professional Journalists gave the authors of the TV Guide article an award, Tom Shales, the TV critic of the *Washington Post* wrote a column rebuking the SPJ.

However, you cannot conclude that the only bad leaks are those that reveal wrongdoing on the part of journalists. We are now seeing important elements of the media working themselves into a lather over the leak of a White House document—a political document, not a national security document. Outrage is being expressed over the fact that in 1980, someone leaked a briefing book prepared for Jimmy Carter prior to his nationally televised debate with Ronald Reagan.

This is being called "debate-gate," and some in the media are trying hard to make it into another Watergate scandal. This leak, we are supposed to agree, was different from leaks to the news media. The beneficiary of the leak was not the *Washington Post* or the *New York Times*. If one of their enterprising reporters had got his hands on the book and had written lengthy stories about it, exposing the strategy of the Carter camp, that would have been treated as a journalistic coup. There would have been no demands for an investigation, no pressure on the journalist to reveal his source.

Since both the *New York Times* and the *Washington Post* were supporting Jimmy Carter, it is quite possible that they would have nobly refrained from publishing the president's debate tactics in advance of the debate. They probably would not have shown any such noble self-restraint had they gotten their hands on the Reagan briefing book.

Since the beneficiary of the leak of the Carter debate briefing book was the Reagan campaign, not a journalist, the media see the leak in an entirely different light. It is no longer a matter of a source rising above such small-minded considerations as loyalty to his employer to satisfy the public's right to know. Now it is a question of thievery and Watergate-style dirty tricks. Those who got the leaked material and used it to their advantage—to help their candidate win the election—are vilified.

This journalistic hypocrisy was brutally exposed by columnist George Will on ABC's "This Week" program. Sam Donaldson, ABC's White House correspondent, and Jody Powell, Carter's former press secretary, wanted to see the culprits brought to justice. When George Will suggested that the same standard be applied to the press, Powell said lamely that the press was different, and Sam Donaldson was momentarily speechless.

July 8, 1983

⦿ 28

It Didn't Start With "Debategate"

The frenetic efforts of the Washington press corps to create a scandal out of the leak of Carter campaign documents may in the end do more to discredit the media than anyone else. There are a lot of journalists who are uneasy about the way this story is being played. Some are downright disgusted. One Washington editor described it as "a non-story." Mr. Arthur Ochs Sulzberger, the chairman of the *New York Times,* said that it appeared to him to be overblown. The Washington bureau chief of a magazine that devoted a great deal of space to the story said he was shocked by the attention that was being given to what everyone knew was routine in all political campaigns.

Meg Greenfield, the editorial page editor of the *Washington Post,* agonized publicly about the media treatment of the story. In a column published in both the *Post* and *Newsweek* magazine, Miss Greenfield said, "...afraid of underplaying, of being caught again, we overplay." She added: "I'm not saying we overplay everything or even that his particular flap may not have ugly dimensions as yet unrevealed, only that there is this anxiety in the journalistic air, this fear of not following a big one to its proper conclusion, of looking the fool."

Miss Greenfield was also troubled by the selectivity of the press in handling matters of this kind. She noted that some of the biggest political scandals had been virtually ignored by the media, while other cases that had ended up not amounting to anything had been commented upon "extravagantly."

Despite all the sound and fury over the briefing book, the evidence so far is that it is about as explosive as a soggy firecracker. The *Washington Post's* news editors obviously don't share Meg Greenfield's concern. On July 7, the *Post* carried four separate stories and two columns by in-house writers about the briefing book story and its ramifications. These stories and columns were found on pages 1, 3, 4, 5, 6, 7, and B1. The author of the main story, Martin Schram, said on CBS's "Nightwatch" program that he did not consider this to be another Watergate. He just thought it was an interesting story, but his editors seem to think that it is one of earthshaking importance. As Miss Greenfield said, "We tend to play it big and then say, 'See, we told you it was big.' "

Despite all the space that the *Post, Newsweek, Time* and others have been giving to a story that was rejected as lacking in news value when it first came to the attention of *Time* magazine two years ago, these publications have not found space to put what happened in perspective. Of course, there have been statements to the effect that some politicians and observers have said that gathering intelligence is commonplace in campaigns, but the major media have not taken the trouble to discuss specific examples that they knew about or could have learned about.

For example, *Time* asked Senator George McGovern what he would have done if he had been offered confidential campaign material from the opposing camp. Sen. McGovern said, "I hope I would have said, 'No, we don't resort to that stuff around here. Send it back.' But I don't know."

Why didn't the reporter simply pick up a copy of Victor Lasky's book, *It Didn't Start With Watergate,* and remind their readers of some of the things that Senator McGovern's campaign workers did back in the 1972 race? Lasky quotes McGovern's deputy press secretary as saying, "Several campaign workers admitted...that they knew our campaign had a spy 'very high up' in the Muskie campaign who had been helpful in 'liberating' some key documents...." He cites evidence that McGovern also had a spy inside the Humphrey camp. He points out that there was even a plan to plant spies on the Republican campaign planes. No wonder Dick Tuck, the veteran Democratic dirty trickster who worked for George McGovern said, "I agree with Reagan on this one. This is certainly much ado about nothing." The reporters know this, but it's not the way they're telling it.

July 15, 1983

⊙ 29

Poll Results You May Have Missed

On "Nightline" on July 13, ABC News delved into the question of whether the news media were making a mountain out of a molehill in the case of the leaked Carter briefing book. Viewers were invited to call one of two special phone numbers to indicate whether they thought the leak of Carter papers to the Reagan campaign should be treated as a major or minor matter by the media and the government.

Some 226,000 viewers took advantage of this offer to tell the network what they thought. Two-thirds—149,000—indicated that they thought this ought to be treated as a minor matter. In doing so they effectively repudiated the way in which this affair has been blown up by much of the media, including ABC News itself.

ABC cautioned that this was not a scientific poll. "Nightline" host Ted Koppel observed that Republicans might be better able to afford the 50 cents to place the call than are Democrats. A person who felt strongly about the matter could call more than once. In order to balance this unscientific survey,

ABC News interviewed 600 people around the country to see how they felt on this same subject. The results were roughly the same. Sixty-one percent felt that the media were overplaying the briefing book story.

The message to the media should have come through loud and clear, but ABC News itself muted it. Even though 226,000 viewers had spent a total of $113,000 to make their views known, and ABC itself had spent a substantial sum to do its scientific survey, the results were not reported on any ABC News program except "Nightline." Only the night owls, the folks who stay up to watch a program that starts at 11:30 P.M., were informed of the results of the ABC poll.

Indeed, to learn the final results of the call-in poll, one had to watch "Nightline" the night after the poll was taken. When those results were given, the host, Ted Koppel, again emphasized the unscientific nature of the poll. He did not mention that these results were in fairly close agreement with the more scientific survey that ABC News had made. The only people who learned about the results of that survey were those who had watched the very end of the "Nightline" program the previous night.

Those who view the media with suspicion will probably conclude that ABC News was not very eager to publicize the fact that its own viewers did not agree with its news judgment about the importance of the case of the leaked briefing book. Those suspicions were probably strengthened by the very unbalanced panels that Ted Koppel had on his program to discuss the case. The night the poll was taken, he interviewed Senator Ernest F. Hollings, one of the candidates for the Democratic presidential nomination, and representatives of three other Democratic presidential candidates. All agreed that the briefing book case was worthy of all the attention the media were giving it. He also had on three reporters, only one of whom thought the coverage had been exaggerated.

Koppel explained that he had tried to get a Republican from the White House or from Congress to appear on the program, but everyone he had approached had declined. The White House press office confirmed that they had refused to make anyone available for the program "because the matter is under investigation." It is hard to criticize Koppel for putting on only Democrats if the Republicans won't talk, but he would have had no trouble finding additional journalists who would have helped put the matter in better perspective.

ABC News did not help its image of fairness the following night when it took up the same question in the "Nightline" time slot, only this time it was a special program called "Viewpoint," also hosted by Ted Koppel. This time the panel consisted of five people, only one of whom was critical of media coverage of the briefing book affair. One of the panelists was Jody Powell, formerly press secretary to Jimmy Carter, who had done much to light the fire under the case. Perhaps the lopsided result of ABC's poll was a reaction to the one-sided treatment of the case by ABC News.

July 22, 1983

"GUNBOAT DIPLOMACY"

"POPULAR LIBERATION FORCE"

30

The Media Blackout of the Good Guys

The polls indicate that the American people are very confused about Central America. Many people are confused about the geography, and even more are confused about the politics. One recent poll indicated that only eight percent of those surveyed knew which side the United States was backing in both El Salvador and Nicaragua.

Who is to blame for this sad state of affairs? It is true that our media have carried a lot of stories about Central America. It is also true that the media have not been very clear about who are the good guys and who are the bad guys in Nicaragua and El Salvador. One reason for this is because writers and editors of some very influential publications think that the good guys are the ones being backed by Cuba and the Soviet Union. Our government, on the other hand, says that they are the bad guys who have to be stopped.

No one has put this more clearly than the foreign editor of the *Washington Post*, Karen DeYoung. Lecturing at the far-left Institute for Policy Studies in Washington a few years ago, Miss

DeYoung said: "Most journalists now, most Western journalists at least, are very eager to seek out guerrilla groups, leftist groups, because you assume that they must be the good guys." Miss DeYoung, when she was covering Nicaragua in 1978 and 1979, was one of those who sought out the guerrillas trying to take over the country. She showed by her stories that she considered them to be the good guys.

Now that Miss DeYoung's "good guys" have been in power in Nicaragua for four years, they have demonstrated that their promises to bring greater freedom and democracy to the country were cynical lies designed to hoodwink the gullible. Miss DeYoung and many of her colleagues in the media don't seem too anxious to call that to public attention. When NBC recently aired a documentary that told the truth about the broken promises of the Sandinistas in Nicaragua, Miss DeYoung, who doesn't normally review television programs, wrote a very critical review of the program for the *Post*.

Several groups concerned about the lack of public understanding about what is happening in Nicaragua put together a very impressive conference in Washington, D.C. on July 19, the fourth anniversary of the seizure of power by the Sandinistas. Speakers included Senator Henry Jackson, Cong. Henry Hyde, Amb. Jeane Kirkpatrick, and a dozen important Nicaraguan exiles. The Nicaraguans included representatives of labor, business, the press, the Nicaraguan Indians, educators, and the freedom fighters. One was Miguel Bolanos Hunter, until very recently a senior intelligence officer in the Sandinista regime.

Bolanos answered those who claim that the Sandinistas are not interfering in El Salvador and other neighboring countries, saying that they began to lay the basis for exporting their revolution as soon as they came to power. He said they had their sights not only on El Salvador, but Honduras, Guatemala, and Costa Rica as well. A high-level defector from the guerrilla forces in El Salvador, Comandante Alejandro Montenegro, told the conference that he had been sent to Cuba for training, via Nicaragua. He said it was the Cubans who were giving the important orders to the guerrillas in El Salvador and that this was one reason for the loss of popular support.

Two Nicaraguan journalists, Humberto Belli and Adrian

Guillen, discussed the loss of press freedom. Teresa Bendana, principal of a girl's school, described the indoctrination of the Cuban-controlled educational system. Her husband, a business leader, discussed the plight of the businessmen. A former member of the Port Workers' Union told what had happened to the workers. They and other speakers made it clear that the Sandinistas have betrayed their promise to every sector of Nicaraguan society.

The next day, the *Washington Post* devoted nearly a page and a half to Nicaragua, but it ignored this conference completely. Instead it gave 19 column inches to a small group in Washington that celebrated the anniversary of the Sandinista victory. The *Washington Times* ran a good story about the conference, but TV ignored it completely, except for C-SPAN, which fed it live to cable systems. No wonder the public is confused.

July 29, 1983

31

Going to the Dogs

Since President Reagan went on the radio to ask for liver donors for a child that would have died without one, the media have had a rash of stories about this remarkable life-saving miracle of modern medicine. None of them has pointed out that these human transplants have become possible only because of experimentation done on dogs. Yes, dogs have died so human beings might live.

There are animal lovers who think this is wrong, but they are in a very small minority. Most people still value human life above animal life. If nothing else, our enormous consumption of beef, pork, lamb and chicken demonstrates that. But the tiny minority is persistent and sometimes gets its way by successful manipulation of the media. This was demonstrated on July 26, when the *Washington Post* ran a front page story headlined, "Military Plan To Shoot Dogs Raises Hackles."

The story revealed that the Uniformed Services University of the Health Sciences planned to shoot dogs with high velocity bullets as part of a program to train military doctors to recognize the wounds and treat them properly. The second paragraph of the story reported that "animal welfare advocates" were outraged and were mobilizing support in Congress to block the program. Indeed, all but one paragraph on the front page was about the opposition to the program.

To find out what the program was all about and how it was being handled, the reader had to jump to the continuation of the story on page A7 and read through the eighth paragraph to learn that the dogs being used in this program were those scheduled to be killed by animal shelters. Two paragraphs later, the reader learned that the dogs would be put to sleep before they were shot, so they would feel no pain. Two paragraphs after that, the reader was told that after being shot the dogs would be given a drug so they would never wake up.

In other words, one had to read nearly to the end of a long story to find out that the perfectly painless killing of the dogs was merely transferred from the animal shelter to the medical teaching laboratory. The story never did clearly explain why the doctors believed this was necessary. It said that the purpose was to enable students to learn to recognize live and dying tissues and to teach them how to treat the wound with the least damage to vital parts. It did not explain clearly that the wounds caused by high velocity weapons used in battle today damage tissue in ways that are hard to recognize unless the doctor has had previous training that could save the lives and limbs of American soldiers.

Accuracy in Media called eighteen dog owners and trainers to see how they felt about using dogs that were slated to die for this kind of humanitarian purpose. All but one said they had no objection to it. Very few of those who had see the front-page article in the *Washington Post* knew of the humane procedures that the Uniformed Services University proposed to follow. Why? Simply because like a great many people they had not bothered to read the part of the story that was continued on the inside page. The *Washington Post* had used the front page for the emotional, inflamatory material. It had buried the information that would have defused and emotions deep down where many people, even those interested in the subject, never got to it.

As a result, the emotions of a lot of people were inflamed.

It was not confined to readers of the *Post*, since the story was picked up by others. One irresponsible radio station suggested that listeners call the Department of the Defense to protest the program. The Pentagon received about 4,000 calls. Secretary of Defense Caspar Weinberger felt the heat. Without consulting with his own experts, including the service surgeon generals, he ordered the program terminated. The *Washington Post* proudly reported this the next day—another feather in its cap. This time it buried the fact that the dogs were to be killed humanely in the very last paragraph. Now Sec. Weinberger says a study will be made. In the end, common sense will probably prevail, with no thanks due to the *Washington Post*.

August 5, 1983

Note: Subsequently we learned that the uniformed services university planned to obtain the dogs from private contractors. It was not specified where they would obtain the animals, but presumably they would have relied mainly on animal shelters. Because of the negative publicity the plan to use dogs was dropped and pigs were substituted.

◉ 32

Fidel Castro's Dirty Tricks

A hot new book is out this month, *Monimbo*, by Arnaud de Borchgrave and Robert Moss. De Borchgrave and Moss, two topflight veteran journalists, have produced an exciting sequel to their previous bestseller, *The Spike*. *The Spike* was about the Soviet KGB and its success in getting disinformation into the mass media of the West. In *Monimbo*, the subject is the Cuban intelligence service, the DGI, and its very dirty tricks. The book is fiction, but like *The Spike* it is based on a lot of research into DGI operations, information that our media have not shown much interest in sharing with the public.

De Borchgrave and Moss present a terrifying scenario of chaos created in this country by Castro's agents. That hasn't happened yet, but *Monimbo* is a warning. It is acknowledged that Castro has infiltrated large numbers of agents into this country. The KGB has delegated many of its tasks to the Cuban DGI because the DGI agents find it easier to become assimilated and gain trust.

There is also no doubt that Castro succeeded in planting in

our midst some very dangerous troublemakers—the hardened criminals who were shipped here during the 1981 Mariel boatlift. We thought that we were doing our humanitarian duty in accepting 125,000 refugees from Cuba—men and women who wanted to be reunited with their families, or those who were willing to abandon everything to escape the drabness and oppression imposed on Cuba by communism.

Castro had other ideas. He was willing to let a lot of the genuine refugees go, but he also put on those boats a collection of Cuba's worst criminals and psychopaths. These thugs figure prominently in *Monimbo* in carrying out unspeakable crimes. In real life they have already created serious problems for Miami and other cities in which they have congregated. They have proven to be more brutal than our home-grown criminals, perhaps reflecting the dehumanizing impact of communism.

Relatively little attention has been given to the problems already created by the Marielista criminals, not to mention the grave potential dangers that de Borchgrave and Moss portray in their new novel. The tendency to gloss over these problems was demonstrated by a segment on the popular CBS program, "60 Minutes," that was recently rebroadcast. "60 Minutes" took up the question of the Marielistas with criminal backgrounds who are being held in the federal penitentiary in Atlanta because the government believes they pose a danger to society.

CBS gave the impression that many of these men were political prisoners in Cuba, or men who had been imprisoned for petty crimes. A lot of attention was given to the views of a federal judge who has ordered many of them to be released. His view is that they have committed no crimes in this country and that therefore the government has no right to jail them. There was nothing on the program that suggested the depravity of these men that comes through in *Monimbo*. The viewer was led to think that the judge, not the Department of Justice, was right.

Two nights earlier, ABC's "20/20" had done a much better job. It had shown the number and ferocity of the crimes committed by the Cuban criminals already released. It showed them proudly displaying their tattoos which are the mark of the professional criminal. Some of the tattoos, ABC noted, identify professional killers. The viewer was left with an appreciation of the efforts of the Justice Department to keep these men behind bars pending their return to Cuba, if that can ever be arranged.

Monimbo also goes into Castro's efforts to flood the United States with narcotics. This is another true story which our media have sadly neglected. The plot may read like fiction, but earlier this year some of the conspirators were convicted in court in Miami. Indicted along with them were the admiral who heads Castro's navy and Castro's former ambassador to Colombia. One of the witnesses for the government testified that he had been sent here during the Mariel boatlift with the assignment of promoting Castro's drug trade. The media paid little attention to all this. Read *Monimbo,* and you'll learn more about Castro's dirty tricks than the media are willing to tell you.

August 12, 1983

33

Should We Abolish Fairness?

The Federal Communications Commission is arousing the wrath of both liberals and conservatives with it efforts to eliminate the rules long in effect that were designed to guard against unfair use of the airwaves. If asked if they wanted news and public affairs programs on radio and television to be fair, surely the overwhelming majority would say yes. And that is what the law now requires. There is a rule called the fairness doctrine that says that when a broadcaster discusses a controversial issue of public importance all sides must be presented.

A subsidiary rule requires that when a personal attack is made on an individual or a group, questioning their integrity, honesty, or like qualities, the target of the attack must be notified and given an opportunity to reply on the air. Still another subsidiary rule says that if a station broadcasts an editorial in favor of a political candidate, it must offer time to that candidate's opponents to reply.

All of these rules have been on the books for many years. While their enforcement has been somewhat ragged, they have served some very important functions. They have acted as a brake on owners of broadcasting licenses who might have been tempted to use their stations to seize political power for themselves or their friends. They have curbed those who might want to use the power that a broadcasting license gives to undermine or destroy personal or political enemies.

The rules have also resulted in greater efforts on the part of broadcast journalists to give both sides of important controversies. They have not produced perfect fairness by any means. Documentaries aired by the three networks have tended to employ what is called "fairness filler." That means that insertion of a little material in an unbalanced documentary that the network can point to and claim that it has covered both sides. This is "token" fairness, but we have also seen a lot more genuine effort to give both sides than we would have seen in the absence of the fairness doctrine. Giving the opposition party an opportunity to put a spokesman on television to reply to a speech by the president is one example that we are all familiar with.

Local stations have tended to be more responsive to demands that they honor the fairness doctrine requirements than have the networks. Individuals who have been attacked on the air have been able to invoke the personal attack rule to get their side of the story told. Groups fighting for an issue have found the fairness doctrine of immense help in getting a hearing on radio and television stations that favored their opponents. Candidates have not had to worry about being confronted in the last days of the campaign with a barrage of free editorial plugs given to their opponents by powerful broadcasters.

This has been an important safety valve in our society. Unfair treatment can generate a lot of anger, and that anger can produce violence or alienation if the injustice persists. Angry voters are not likely to be pacified by the argument that they must put up with rank unfairness on the air because that is what the Founding Fathers decreed. The Founding Fathers never addressed the issue, and they would certainly be appalled to see how our courts have misconstrued their intentions over the last fifty years.

Unfortunately, President Reagan's appointees to the FCC all seem to be doctrinaire disciples of the late Supreme Court

Justice, Hugo Black, who pioneered the simpleminded interpretation of the first amendment that has resulted in such dubious blessings as the gross pornography that has flooded our country. They would like to get rid of the fairness doctrine altogether (and also their mandate to keep obscenity off the air), but they can't repeal the law.

They have virtually halted enforcement of the law, and now they propose to wipe out the rules that put the brakes on personal attacks and editorials endorsing candidates. If you favor fairness on the air, you ought to tell the President how you feel about this.

August 19, 1983

 34

CBS Aids the Enemy and Pays Them to Boot

Belatedly and timidly the White House has begun to criticize publicly the media coverage of Central America. Boldly and blatantly that coverage has become more and more hostile to the policies of the U.S. government and more favorable to the communists in Nicaragua and El Salvador.

One of the more blatant demonstration of slanting the coverage to denigrate the U.S. government and make the communist side appear to be in the right appeared on the CBS Evening News on August 3. Our government had revealed that a Soviet ship, the Alexander Ulyanov, was carrying cargo that included military hardware to Nicaragua. The hardware was said to include helicopters. Considerable attention was focused on this vessel, especially after a U.S. destroyer encountered the Ulyanov at sea and questioned its captain as to its cargo and its destination.

The Ulyanov docked at the Nicaraguan port of Corinto on August 3. Western reporters were barred from the port and were unable to undertake any personal investigation of the ship's cargo. The Soviets and Nicaraguans had denied that the ship was carrying military equipment, but they were not willing to let American or other reporters verify that claim.

Rather than draw the not unreasonable conclusion that our government was correct in its description of the cargo, since the Nicaraguans obviously had something to hide, CBS took a different approach. It purchased videotape shot aboard the Ulyanov by a Cuban camera crew and used this on its evening news program. Showing the filmed shots of a bulldozer and a large container, CBS correspondent Richard Wagner said: "As Western journalists continued to be barred from Corinto by Nicaraguan authorities, CBS News purchased this videotape today. Nothing of a military nature is evident aboard the Ulyanov in these scenes shot by a source friendly to Nicaragua."

Wagner went on to say that the ship had been "the object of much attention since President Reagan said it was carrying helicopters and other military equipment." He said, "The Soviets have consistently denied sending military supplies to Nicaragua. Corinto is this country's major port city. These scenes from the purchased videotape show East German and Soviet vessels at the main pier. Again, only non-military cargo is seen. The Nicaraguan government also denies military equipment is sent here from the Soviet Union." Correspondent Wagner then concluded: "Despite the denials, it's clear that the Nicaraguan army has lots of Soviet military hardware. How it gets here is less clear."

That seems to suggest that Mr. Wagner was satisfied, on the basis of the videotapes, that the Alexander Ulyanov had not transported military cargo to Nicaragua as had been charged by President Reagan. Why CBS News or anyone else should have reached such a conclusion is beyond comprehension, since Wagner conceded that the Soviet military hardware is getting to Nicaragua. Does CBS think that it is being shipped in by air?

Only after Government officials made it known that the videotape CBS had used to contradict the President was of Cuban origin did CBS admit that it had bought the tape from the Cubans. Why was the source not honestly described when the footage was shown on the air? The answer seems obvious. The Cubans had shot the tape for one purpose—to disprove

Reagan's charges. But few Americans would be willing to accept tape shot by Cubans as any kind of proof that the Ulyanov was not carrying military equipment. Since CBS News was making the point that the Cubans wanted made, the source of the film had to be concealed from the viewers if it was to have any credibility.

Our embassy in Managua had reported that CBS had paid "an astronomical price" for the Cuban tape. The *New York Post* quoted a CBS official as saying that the price was only $2,500. One CBS official said the tape was used because "it was the only stuff around and it was a major news story." It is bad enough that CBS is willing to air Cuban propaganda. Does it have to pay Cuba to boot?

August 26, 1983

35

CBS: The Negative Network

The August 27 issue of *TV Guide* magazine carries a devastating demonstration of the anti-Reagan bias of CBS News. The author, John Weisman, analyzed the evening news broadcasts of all three television networks for the week beginning May 1 to see how they were covering President Reagan and his administration. He came up with good evidence that the network news is not all the same. Weisman found a very significant difference between CBS News and its rivals, ABC and NBC. As far as the Reagan administration is concerned, CBS can be called "the negative network."

Classifying items on the Reagan administration as positive, negative or neutral, Weisman found that 52 percent of the CBS items were negative and only 10 percent were positive. The rest, were neutral. NBC was credited with only 10 percent negative and ABC had 12 percent negative. Both NBC and ABC were predominantly neutral in their reporting, but NBC was found to have 26 percent of the items aired favorable to Reagan, and ABC was credited with 18 percent of its items in the positive category.

This is an astonishing difference, and it calls for some explanation. Howard Stringer, the executive producer of the CBS Evening News, explained it this way: "I think the president and the White House would rather have a straightforward record of the president's activities. We don't do that. We don't do a presidential diary. We're closer to analysis."

Dan Rather, the CBS News anchorman, put it this way: "Part of our job—whether it's a Democratic or Republican administration—is to say to our audience, 'All right, this is what the president says is happening. Now we're going to go out and see whether, in fact, this *is* what is happening.' When it is, we say so. When it isn't, we say so."

That isn't quite the way it works, however. Take the case of the Soviet ship, the Alexander Ulyanov, that according to President Reagan was carrying military equipment to Nicaragua a month ago. In an effort to show that what the president said was happening was not so, CBS purchased some videotape shot aboard the Ulyanov by a Cuban camera crew. That was shown on the CBS Evening News to demonstrate that Reagan had been wrong, since the Cuban videotape did not show any military cargo. CBS did not tell the viewers that it had acquired the tape from the Cubans. The folks at CBS News aren't dumb. They knew that if they described the source of the tape as Cuban it would have had no credibility, and the effort to show that the president had been wrong would have failed.

Let's examine this against the standards for journalists that Van Gordon Sauter, the president of CBS News, proclaimed in a speech to the National Press Club on June 8. "The first law," said Mr. Sauter, "is that the journalist shall never dare to set down that which is false." In this case, CBS didn't say anything that was false, but it violated Mr. Sauter's second rule: "that he shall never dare to conceal the truth."

CBS News concealed what it knew to be a very relevant piece of information—that the tape had been shot by a Cuban camera crew and that CBS had paid the Cubans money for it. Gene Mater, a CBS News vice president, claimed that the Cuban camera crew was a freelance group that did not work for any official Cuban agency. It is hard to imagine that Gene Mater really believes that Fidel Castro permits freelance Cuban journalists to roam around the world. His explanation became even more hilarious when he said that the viewers might have been confused if CBS had said the tape was acquired from a freelance Cuban crew, not knowing whether it was Miami Cubans or Havana Cubans. Can't you just see the Sandinistas and the Soviets permitting anti-Castro Cubans to film aboard the Ulyanov when they wouldn't let journalists from non-communist countries even get near the port?

Mr. Sauter's final law was "that there shall be no suspicion in his work of either favoritism or malice." The favoritism and malice literally dripped from this news item. A Cuban videotape, which CBS was ashamed to identify, was actually used to discredit our chief executive. The fact that CBS has advanced ridiculous excuses to justify this journalistic disgrace and has not fired those responsible for it suggests that the malice is policy at CBS News. No wonder it comes through at the negative network.

September 2, 1983

⊙ 36

Let's "Pariahtize" the Soviet Union

The deliberate murder by the Soviet Union of Congressman Larry McDonald and 268 other innocent human beings on the Korean Airlines jumbo jet has evoked bitter, worldwide condemnation of the Soviets. Everyone agrees that they behaved barbarically, but there is little agreement as to what retribution should be visited upon them. Suggestions have ranged from breaking off diplomatic relations and cutting off trade to simply insisting that the Kremlin make an apology.

The Soviets have been getting away with vile deeds of this type for decades. The evidence is strong that Andropov and his KGB were behind the attempt to murder the Pope. He was one of the masterminds in the crushing of the Hungarian freedom fighters in 1956, but little things like that have not stopped world leaders and even distinguished American senators from rushing to the Kremlin to shake his blood-stained hand.

The people of the Free World have short memories. The erection of the Berlin Wall, the crushing of the Hungarian and Czech revolts, the torture of Soviet dissidents in psychiatric hospitals, the invasion of Afghanistan, the smashing of Solidarity and the imprisonment of Lech Walesa are only a few of the many communist atrocities that aroused world emotions for a brief period of time. Naive western observers in each case have asked with amazement how the Kremlin could do things that so damaged the reputation of the Soviet Union. The masters of the Kremlin have shown little concern for world public opinion. Experience has taught them that no matter what horrible deed they perpetrate, the world will soon forget and forgive.

We are soon to have our collective conscience pricked by yet another film based on the case of Julius and Ethel Rosenberg, who were executed thirty years ago for giving our atomic bomb secrets to the Soviets. They were guilty as sin, but the communist propaganda apparatus has labored tirelessly for three decades to blacken America's image with the lie that they were innocent victims of a gigantic conspiracy. We do nothing comparable with the truly monstrous crimes of the Soviet Union and other communist countries.

The difference is explained by the fact that the communists have a far better grasp of the art of influencing world opinion than we do. It was in their interest that the My Lai massacre be widely publicized and that its memory be perpetuated. It received enormous attention in the American press. If you ask a college audience today how many have heard of the My Lai massacre almost every hand will go up. If you ask how many have heard of the Hue massacre, the cold-blooded murder of 3,000 civilians by the communists in the Vietnamese city of Hue in 1968, no one will raise his hand. It was not in the communist interest that the Hue massacre be publicized and remembered—and it wasn't.

There is no reason to think it will be any different with the KAL flight 007 massacre, unless the civilized world decides that the time has come to turn the tables on the communists. If any country in the world deserves to be treated as a pariah it is the Soviet Union. It oppresses its own people, the people in neighboring countries that it has subjugated, it directly and indirectly supports a worldwide terror network, and it is the sworn enemy of freedom everywhere. Its system stifles creativity and creates shortages of consumer goods wherever it is introduced.

We hear a lot about how we need to understand the Soviets. A group of New England editors has journeyed to Moscow and has invited their counterparts to visit New England to promote understanding. The Maine schoolgirl, Samantha Smith, went to the Soviet Union, and her trip was given great media coverage. The message was that the Russians are just like us.

This is phony understanding. The understanding we need is that the Soviets are ruled by cruel, ruthless men who don't share our Judeo-Christian values. The KAL massacre is one more proof of that. That is the message that our media need to focus on.

September 9, 1983

◉ 37

The "Knock-America" Media

Media coverage of the Korean Air Lines massacre has demonstrated to all but a tiny fraction of the American people that the Soviet Union knowingly shot a jetliner out of the sky and killed 269 people. A poll taken by ABC's "Nightline" showed that only three percent of those surveyed thought the Soviet action had been justified.

However, there have been some sour notes in the media coverage. Some of our reporters and editors have developed an attitude of mistrusting anything that is said by the U.S. government. When the massacre story first broke, the two most influential newspapers in the country, the *New York Times* and the *Washington Post,* demonstrated their reluctance to believe our government by heading their stories, "U.S. says" the Soviets shot down the airliner. The *New York Times* was still exhibiting that caution the day after Ambassador Jeane Kirkpatrick played for the U.N. Security Council the tape recording of the Soviet pilot's comments as he committed the crime. The *Times* said, "A hushed and intent Security Council today heard 11 minutes of the tape recorded voice that the United States said was that of the Soviet fighter pilot. . . . '' That kind of treatment subtly conveys the message, ''The government is saying it, but we don't necessarily believe it.

Perhaps that is only an excess of caution, but caution was thrown to the winds by some papers in their treatment of the story that the Soviets may have shot down the airliner because they confused it with a U.S. Air Force reconnaissance plane. This story first appeared in the *Washington Post* on September 3. It was reported as something that unidentified analysts suspected. The basis of the suspicion turned out to be very flimsy, and if a few more questions had been asked before the story was printed, the reporter and his editors should have realized that they did not have a story worthy of the prominent play they gave it on page one.

These suspicions turned out to be based on the fact that an RC-135 reconnaissance plane had intersected the route flown by the Korean 747 as the airliner was flying southwest toward the Kamchatka Peninsula and the RC-135 was flying northeast over international waters along the peninsula. Both planes were tracked by Soviet radar, as were numerous other aircraft that were flying in that area at that time. Both planes had filed flight plans with the International Civil Aviation Organization (ICAO). The Soviets presumably had those plans, since they get them from ICAO. To have confused the two planes, the Soviet radar operators would have had to assume that KAL Flight 7 had turned right instead of left, flying not toward Japan, but northward along the route taken regularly by the reconnaissance plane, while the RC-135 also veered off course, reversing its direction.

That would be a bit much. Actually, the Soviets tracked the Korean plane for two and a half hours, and before shooting it down, the pilot had established visual contact with it. In the moonlit night, the pilot could not have mistaken the huge jumbo jet, with its distinctive humpback, for the much smaller RC-135, which is a converted Boeing 707. Even if the pilot had not been able to see the plane clearly, he had it on his radar. Experts say that the size of the jumbo jet on the fighter plane radar would clearly have distinguished it from the smaller plane.

President Reagan debunked the mis-identification theory in his televised address to the nation. He pointed out that the RC-135 had returned to Alaska and was on the ground an hour before the jetliner was shot down. But some skeptical journalists were hard to convince. Bill Plante of CBS News went on the air right after the president to say: "They keep insisting that there is no other conclusion that can be drawn but that the Soviets shot that airliner out of the air deliberately, but a number of us keep asking if that is necessarily the case. We think it may still be possible that a mistake was made. And that is a question that the administration simply hasn't answered."

No wonder White House spokesman Larry Speakes criticized reporters that "search for some Soviet mistake that would apologize for them or mitigate their responsibility."

September 16, 1983

⊙ 38

Rather Blows His
"Nice Guy" Image

Dan Rather, the anchorman on the CBS Evening News, is trying very hard to project the public image of a decent, dignified, nice guy. Big money is riding on his ability to convince the viewing audience that he is credible, respectable, and even lovable. The anchorman is believed to have a lot of influence on the ratings of the news programs. If the viewers don't like the anchorman, ratings will suffer, and that costs the network advertising revenue.

When Rather succeeded Walter Cronkite on the CBS Evening News, the ratings slipped. The viewers apparently didn't feel quite as comfortable with Dan as they had with the avuncular Walter Cronkite. But then Dan accidentally discovered that he projected a warmer image if he wore a pullover sweater. The ratings recovered, and CBS again rose to the top of the heap in the evening news ratings war.

CBS was understandably nervous this spring when Dan Rather had to go to court in Los Angeles to defend himself against a libel suit. A young black doctor, Carl Galloway, had charged that Rather had slandered him back in 1979 on "60 Minutes." Rather had gone on the air with the charge that Dr. Galloway had signed a false medical report that was purportedly to be used to collect a false insurance claim. That's a felony.

Dr. Galloway was able to demonstrate that his name had been forged on the medical report, and he denied having anything to do with the insurance scam. He testified that neither Dan Rather nor anyone from CBS had checked with him about that false medical report he was supposed to have signed before Rather accused him of committing a felony before the 40 million or so viewers that watch "60 Minutes."

Rather and his producer, Steve Glauber, contended that they had placed two phone calls to Galloway's office, leaving the message that Dan Rather wanted to talk to him. They didn't hear from Dr. Galloway, and they went on the air with the story assuming that he had really signed that report. Rather testified that it was his experience that the guilty generally don't call back. Dr. Galloway denied ever having received any messages to call Dan Rather.

A television journalist, Steve Wilson, who is working for a new syndicated program called "Breakaway," recently turned the tables on Dan Rather. Wilson was doing a segment for "Breakaway" about the Galloway case, which had resulted in a jury verdict in favor of Rather and CBS. He wanted to interview Rather, and he telephoned him three times. Rather didn't call back. Wilson sent him a registered letter. He got no reply to that either.

Finally, Wilson resorted to a technique that "60 Minutes" had made famous—the ambush interview. He and his camera crew waited outside CBS News headquarters in New York until Dan Rather appeared. Going up to Rather, Wilson said, "Could I see you for just a moment? I've called your office three times. I've sent you a registered letter. . . . I don't know how else to do it."

Rather half-grinned, put his hand on Steve Wilson's shoulder, and said to a member of the camera crew, "Get that microphone right up, will you?" With Wilson's cameras rolling and the microphone right in front of his face, Rather then said, "----

you. You got it? Clearly?'' He had been recorded uttering a four-letter obscenity that nice guys are not supposed to use, at least not in public.

Wilson recognized that he had on video tape an interview with CBS's eight-million-dollar man that just might be worth airing. Rather apparently realized after a while that he might have shot himself in the foot by his rude and vulgar conduct. He called Wilson to apologize and to offer to give him an interview. Wilson was not interested. On September 8, Rather sent Wilson an abject written apology. He said, ''I mistook who you were and what you were doing. That was inexcusable, rude and un-Christian behavior for which I am remorseful.'' Wilson was unmoved. ''Breakway'' aired Wilson's ''interview'' with Rather, bleeping out the obscenity. Millions finally saw the real Dan Rather.

September 23, 1983

39

The Big Lie Works

Thomas Jefferson once said that we could safely tolerate error as long as truth was free to combat it. That idea has been the foundation on which we have based our faith that the freedom we give our press does us no harm if it does encourage the dissemination of a fair amount of erroneous information. We are confident that in the end the truth will prevail.

In the wake of the Korean Air Lines massacre, much of the comment in the media has suggested that there is a good deal of doubt in the land that the truth will prevail over the patently false Soviet version of what transpired in the skies over Kamchatka and Sakhalin Island on September 1. It is not that the communist lies are at the moment being bought by the American people. Quite the contrary. Even the knee-jerk communist apologists are having a hard time swallowing the line that KAL Flight 7 was on a spy mission for the United States and that it was flying without navigation lights and maneuvering to escape the supersonic Soviet fighters that went up to intercept it. It is rather difficult to overcome the evidence to the contrary pre-

served in the tape recordings of the voice of the pilot who perpetrated the massacre.

But what is bothering many commentators is the realization that after a clumsy beginning, the Kremlin has cranked up
its propaganda machine. It has directed it to try to undo the
damage already done and to try to convince the world that Un-
cle Sam, not the Soviet Union is the villain in this case. A hope-
less task, you may say. The evidence against them is too
overwhelming. Their story is too burdened with absurdities and
contradictions to be taken seriously by anyone.

But past experience with communist propaganda successes
ought to temper such optimism. Truth usually does win out
over error when the two are equally free to compete in the arena
of information and ideas. But as Adolf Hitler pointed out and
demonstrated, lies can overwhelm truth if they are sufficiently
audacious and are repeated often enough. The bigger the lie,
the better the chance of getting it accepted, in Hitler's view.

The communists have shown themselves to be the masters
of the Big Lie, and they are counting on it to work for them
again in the case of the Korean Air Lines massacre. Some of
our journalists offered them a little lie as a way of getting off the
hook—the lie that they mistook the huge jumbo jetliner for a
U.S. Air Force reconnaissance plane. The Soviet propagandists
toyed with that idea, but only briefly. It didn't suit their purposes. It made them look incompetent to claim to have made
such a stupid mistake, and the blame would fall entirely on
them. This scenario would not permit them to convince the
gullible that it was really the United States that was at fault.

Therefore, they opted for the Big Lie that KAL Flight 7
was on a spy mission for the United States, which made it fair
game for their interceptors. Since the plane and all aboard were
irretrievably lost, it would be impossible to prove that it wasn't
carrying electronic monitoring gear, cameras and spies. Of
course, the communists had no evidence that it was carrying
any of those things, but the Big Lie doesn't depend on evidence
for its success. It depends on repetition.

The Big Lie was given a magnificent send-off at the media
extravaganza in Moscow on September 9, presided over by
Marshal Nikolai Ogarkov, who said: "It has been proven irre-

futably that the intrusion of the South Korean airlines plane into Soviet airspace was a deliberately, thoroughly planned intelligence operation." Marshal Ogarkov had no proof, irrefutable or otherwise, to back up that charge. That night, one of Radio Moscow's slickest propagandists, Vladimir Posner, was invited to appear on ABC's "Nightline." He repeated over and over that the plane was on a spy mission. He produced no proof either, but he wasn't laughed off the air.

On September 13, an influential syndicated columnist, Joseph Kraft, virtually exonerated the Soviets, saying that they had convinced him that the attack on the airliner "was not an act of deliberate terror." Kraft had been convinced by the now-abandoned little lie of misidentification. The Soviet success with him augurs well for their Big Lie campaign.

September 30, 1983

● 40

ABC Weighs in on
Nuclear Debate

ABC is planning to air a horror movie on November 20, a horror movie with a message. It is called "The Day After," and it is a fictional account of what would happen to Kansas City if a nuclear war broke out and a city in the heartland of America was subjected to a Soviet nuclear attack. The movie is said to be a vivid portrayal of the aftermath of such an attack, including scenes of destruction, burned bodies, victims of radiation, burns and blast.

Nicholas Meyer, the director of the film, says that it takes no political stand. A spokesman for ABC says the film has a message—that nuclear war is horrible. That is a message that hardly needs restating. I don't know of anyone who has believed otherwise since the first nuclear bomb was dropped on Hiroshima.

The question is why has ABC spent so much money—one report, which ABC refuses to confirm or deny, says it cost $7 million—on a film that tells us what we already know. The ABC spokesman also refused to confirm or deny a press report that as of the third week in September the network had been unable to sell a single advertising spot for the movie. He did say, however, that ABC considered the movie so important that they would air it even if they didn't sell any advertising to pay for the time.

That suggests that ABC's entertainment division is getting into the not-for-profit message business. This probably won't delight the ABC shareholders, but it is bringing joy to the hearts of the advocates of a nuclear freeze and other anti-nuke types on the eve of the deployment of Pershing II and cruise missiles in Western Europe. The perpetrators of the Korean Air Lines massacre, the peace-loving rulers of the Soviet Union, have been busily sirring up demonstrations against the deployment of the Pershing missiles in Europe for many months. They have found thousands of people in Europe and in this country who were susceptible to the argument that we will run a great risk of nuclear war if we proceed with the plans to deploy those missiles in Europe. Strangely, these same people didn't seem to notice when the Soviets deployed their SS-20 missiles aimed at Western Europe. They seem to forget that the Pershings are NATO's answer to this new Soviet threat.

In this case the Soviet propagandists have shrewdly diverted attention from their own massive buildup of nuclear weapons by focusing their propaganda campaign on the unspeakable horrors of nuclear war. Who can argue that nuclear war is good? Who will not shudder at the prospect of this country being devastated by a nuclear attack? One of the groups that has taken the lead in the propaganda offensive has been the Physicians for Social Responsibility, which has invited Soviet doctors to this country to help convince us of the horrors of nuclear war. This organization distributes a movie called "The Last Epidemic," which discusses the horrible consequences of a nuclear conflict.

Josh Baran and Diane Eagle, two anti-nuclear activists associated with a group called "Target Kansas City," say that ABC has handed the anti-nuclear movement a wonderful opportunity with its new movie, "The Day After." Baran says that the ABC movie is similar to "The Last Epidemic," but he points out that it will reach many more people. *Nuclear Times* magazine quotes him as saying, "The only way to reach people is through television. The time and money spent to make this film would take the entire peace movement's budget of $20 million. We have to take advantage of the free time." Baran estimates that a single showing of the ABC movie will reach ten or twenty times as many people as would ever see "The Last Epidemic."

An ABC spokesman denied any knowledge of the enthusiasm expressed by the anti-nuclear types over the ABC movie. Can it be that they are really unaware that the pro-freeze movement is planning vigils and marches in association with the showing of the film? *Nuclear Times* says that the anti-nuclear groups are planning "to turn a television commercial event into an educational event on our own terms." But it won't be a commercial event if the advertisers refuse to shell out the money to pay for it.

October 7, 1983

41

Kamchatka Is Not Vietnam

The Korean Air Lines massacre has brought forth a lot of theories and speculation about what happened on the night of September 1 when a Soviet interceptor sent 269 people to a watery grave off Sakhalin Island. Some of it is too bizarre to be taken seriously, but one article that casts doubts on what our government has said has been taken seriously by a number of editors around he country. It has appeared in many big papers, and it was enthusiastically quoted by the leftwing *Village Voice* in its October 4 issue.

As we know, an Air Force RC-135 reconnaissance plane was flying off the coast of the Kamchatka Peninsula at about the same time that KAL Flight 7 was veering off course and heading for the peninsula, which is Soviet territory. The article contends that the RC-135 was monitoring all the Soviet activity on the ground and in the air that related to the airliner's intrusion into Soviet airspace. The authors dispute President Reagan's statement that the RC-135 had returned to its base in Alaska more than one hour before the Korean airliner was shot down over 1,000 miles away. Identifying themselves as former crew members on an RC-135, they say this is misleading because they knew that one RC-135 is always relieved by another, so that one of these reconnaissance planes is constantly on station.

The authors also contend that the RC-135 was linked to "the most sophisticated communication network in the world, permitting the instantaneous reporting of tactical intelligence to the highest levels of government, including the president, from any location in the world." They say, "A message intended for the president is required to be in his hands no more than 10 minutes after the actual time of transmission."

The authors ask why these capabilities of the RC-135 "were never used in an attempt to head off the tragedy." They suggest that the government is covering up important information that would provide the answers to these and other questions.

The fact that papers like the *Denver Post* and the *Chicago Sun-Times* printed this article prominently gave added weight to he doubts raised by the authors about the truth of what the U.S. government has said about the massacre. The article first appeared in the *Denver Post* on September 13 and was then syndicated to other papers around the country by the Los Angeles Times-Washington Post News Service.

Chuck Green, the editor at the *Denver Post* who was responsible for running the story, said that he verified the claim of the two authors, T. Edward Eskelson and Tom Bernard, that they had been crewmen on RC-135 flights out of Okinawa during the Vietnam War. He said he made no effort to verify the truth of what they said about the capabilities of the RC-135 and the way in which the planes are used, because he assumed that this was classified information which the Air Force would refuse to discuss.

The most obvious flaw in the article was that the authors were basing their claims on what they knew of the RC-135 reconnaissance planes and their mission during the Vietnam war. The note identifying them said only that they had flown missions out of Okinawa, without giving the dates. It turns out that both were enlisted men who flew on the planes as Vietnamese linguists in the year 1970. They made the mistake of thinking that Kamchatka in 1983 was the same as Vietnam in 1970. The readers were not told that their information was 13 years out of date.

The RC-135 that was off the coast of Kamchatka on September 1 was there to monitor a specific Soviet missile test. The test was scrubbed, and it returned to its base in Alaska. It was on the ground when the airliner was shot down. In Vietnam, the planes were used to help protect our fighters and bombers over Vietnam. Around the clock deployment may have been the rule at times. That is not true today. There was ample reason to question the outdated expertise of Bernard and Eskelson and check their doubt-casting claims. Unfortunately that was not done. The readers and the nation were badly served.

October 14, 1983

42

How The *Washington Post* Got Jim Watt

A *Washington Post* reporter named Howard Kurtz recently wrote that on each of the nine times this year that his stories had brought about the resignation of a Reagan administration official one of his colleagues stuck a small picture of a fish to the bulletin board above Kurtz's desk. Kurtz said that his success in bringing about resignations gave him the feeling of having done a public service.

On October 9, the *Post* got a big fish, Secretary of Interior James Watt. The *Post* can rightfully claim much of the responsibility for bringing Watt down. It was clear from the day it ran the story of Watt's jocular comment that his coal leasing commission included "a black, a woman, two Jews and a cripple" that the hit men at the *Post* had Jim Watt in their sights. The *Post* played the story big, running it prominently on page one. To make sure that everyone saw the offending statement that was the cause of all the fuss, they set it in big, bold type and boxed it as a "read-out," something one rarely sees in a *Washington Post* news story.

From then on until Watt resigned hardly a day passed that the *Post* didn't carry a story or column about the Watt affair. The remark the secretary had made was repeated over and over again in these articles, almost always omitting the sentence with which Watt had ended his description of the commission, "And we have talent." It was important to drop that sentence down the memory hole, since it conflicted with the assertions so frequently found in the *Post* that Watt was speaking disparagingly of the members of the commission.

The coverage by the *Post* was in sharp contrast with that of the *New York Times,* which had reported Secretary Watt's remark on page A15, using a UPI story that bore the headline: "Watt Apologizes for Words About Coal Panel." The *Post*'s page-one headline had read: "Watt's Off-the-Cuff Remark Sparks a Storm of Criticism."

The story in the *Times* which had also been available to the *Post* from UPI, made it clear that Watt's remark did not reflect any bigotry on the part of the speaker. It quoted Prof. David Linowes, the chairman of the commission, who is Jewish and a Democrat, as saying: "I know he has a sense of humor. If the remarks were made by a bigot, I would have been offended. His track record shows a wholesome record in dealing with other people." The *Post* reported that Linowes had said that Watt's remark "may strike me as of less concern than it strikes others" because he knew from experience that Watt did not have a track record of bigotry. But the emphasis was on the reaction of those who were offended by the remark, including a statement by a liberal Democratic congressman who said he was "disgusted and appalled" by Watt's "gross insensitivity."

The *Times* virtually dropped the Watt story after September 25, running no editorials or angry columns denouncing Watt as a bigot. It did run a story reporting that Watt was highly popular in the West, even with Democratic governors. Not until October 10 did the *Times* report on the pressures that had been generated in Washington to force Watt's resignation. That story concluded that while Watt had been toppled by "a few ill-chosen words," what really did him in was the drastic change in policies that he introduced and the opposition that generated.

The *Washington Post,* however, portrayed James Watt as a

bigoted, prejudiced man. One of the paper's inhouse columnists, Judy Mann, wrote a particularly nasty column that appeared on September 23 in which she suggested that Watt was a white, Christian male who was racist, sexist and anti-semitic. She described him as "a well-poisoner of the first order" who "doesn't understand that we're all in this together." She said, "As far as he's concerned, the good guys are the white Christian male Americans...."

Post editorial page editor Meg Greenfield, in a signed column, accused Watt of "coarseness of mind and sniggering contempt." In an editorial after the resignation, the *Post* conceded that none of the words uttered by Watt were offensive, but it said they had "connotations" and "everybody knew what these were." Everybody who knows Jim Watt denies these charges of bigotry. The *Post* know it, but it was out for blood, not for truthful reporting.

October 21, 1983

43

Another Communist Atrocity Downplayed

Here is a scenario for you. President Reagan, accompanied by a large entourage that includes his chief of staff, James Baker, Secretary of State George Shultz, Secretary of Commerce Malcolm Baldrige, the Chairman of the Council of Economic Advisers, Martin Feldstein, and the Chairman of the Joint Chiefs of Staff, Gen. John W. Vessey, visits Mexico City. While there, he is scheduled to participate in a wreath-laying ceremony together with all of the above. All these dignitaries, with the exception of the president, are gathered at the memorial awaiting the arrival of President Reagan. The American ambassador, John Gavin, arrives in his car, takes his place, and immediately there is a terrific explosion. The roof is blown off the building, and bodies are strewn all over the area.

President Reagan is not harmed, since he had not yet arrived at the site, but 16 members of his party, including all the high officials listed above, with the exception of Gen. Vessey, who is mortally wounded, lie dead. All told, 19 people are dead and at least 48 are wounded. It appears that the president was spared only because the person who detonated the radio-activated bomb pressed the button when Ambassador Gavin arrived, thinking that he was the president. The intent of the plotters was clearly to kill the president and all of the key aides who were accompanying him.

It is not hard to imagine the outrage that would sweep this country, and, indeed, the world, if anything resembling this actually happened. The story would dominate our newspapers and broadcast media for weeks. The most intensive investigation would immediately be launched to determine who was responsible. The suspicion would fall upon communist terrorists, and our people would be reminded of other similar atrocities inspired and perpetrated by the communists—the Korean Air Lines massacre, the attempted assassination of the pope, the murder of former Italian premier Aldo Moro, to name only a few recent examples. If the evidence pointed strongly to the involvement of, say, Cuba in the grisly murder the demand for retributive action would be overwhelming.

The scenario is patterned after what actually did happen in Rangoon, Burma on October 9, only the target of the attack was not President Reagan, but President Chun Doo Hwan of the Republic of Korea. He escaped injury, but his cabinet officers and aides were brutally murdered by the bombs that had been planted in the roof of the Martyr's Mausoleum in Rangoon.

Outrage did sweep South Korea. The Koreans, who have had long experience with the terrorist attacks of the brutal communist regime that tyrannizes their brothers and sisters in North Korea, had no doubt who was responsible for this latest incredible atrocity. They recalled that in 1968, a specially trained team of North Korean assassins had come within an ace of murdering President Chung Hee Park.

Evidence confirming South Korean suspicions has come to light. It was found that there had been three bombs planted in the roof of the Burmese mausoleum, and one had failed to detonate. It was similar in design to bombs that the North Koreans had used elsewhere, and the detonating equipment was identical to that regularly used by North Korean terrorists. Soon the Burmese apprehended three Koreans who appeared to be trying to make their way to the sea. One threw a grenade at the police as they tried to search his bag. He was shot and killed. A second fled and blew off his arm in a suicide attempt, something Korean terrorists faced with capture are supposed to do. The third is now in police custody. Unofficial sources said all three were North Koreans.

The outrage felt in Korea has not been reflected in the American media, which have said almost nothing about North Korea and the evidence that it was to blame. The very day the three North Koreans were apprehended, the *New York Times* carried a big story that started off by saying that some diplomats doubted North Korea was involved. It appeared that the *Times* and some others in our big media were anxious to avoid exciting more anti-communist passions just when the American people were forgetting the Korean Air Lines massacre.

October 28, 1983

◉ 44

Grenada Was an Important First

In the thousands of words written and broadcast about Grenada by our media, one important fact has been ignored. This is the first time in the 66 years since the communists seized control of Russia that an entrenched communist regime with full control over the military, police and press has been overthrown. Assuming that Grenada can be kept free, Ronald Reagan will be the first American president to have demonstrated that communist revolutions are not irreversible. That should spark hope in the victims of communism throughout the world, just as it strikes fear into the hearts of communist oppressors. They have to begin to wonder if the dominoes could fall the other way.

It is clear that the American people overwhelmingly welcome the firm action President Reagan took to achieve this result. An ABC News poll taken after the president's address to the nation on October 27 found that 86 percent supported the president on Grenada. No one polled the media elite to see how they felt, but it appeared clear from the content and tone of the reporting that an enormous gap had opened up between the people of this country and our media elite—those who work for our national media organs. Three-quarters of those polled said they agreed with the statement that the Grenada action made them feel good because it shows that America can use its power to protect its own interests.

These poll results are supported by the calls to the White House. After the president's speech Thursday night, the White House switch board was swamped with calls until well after midnight and again Friday morning. The tabulation of positive and negative calls was not immediately available, but I was told that the calls were overwhelmingly supportive of the president. Even before the president spoke, the White House received over 7,000 calls on Grenada, and nearly three-fourths of them were positive.

The overwhelming support of the American people is almost the mirror image of the media reaction, which was overwhelmingly negative. Papers such as the *New York Times* and the *Washington Post* gave a great deal of space to critics of the U.S. action. The *Post* ran big stories about the criticism of the action from Cuba, Nicaragua, the Soviet Union, the U.K., the United Nations and the Organization of American States. As for American reaction, the *Post* quoted two Republicans and two Democrats who endorsed the president's action, and it quoted six Democrats who were critical. This paper also ran a story impugning the accuracy of Reagan's claim that the action had been necessary to protect the Americans on Grenada. The headline read: "Americans in Grenada, Calling Home, Say They Were Safe Before Invasion."

The *New York Times'* coverage was similar. It quoted two Republicans and one Democrat who supported the president, and four Democrats and two Republicans who were critical. Both papers ran critical editorials. The *Washington Times,* a conservative paper, reported on page one that most Congressional leaders were supportive of the action, and it cited statements by both the Democratic and Republican leadership, as well as supportive statements by leading conservatives outside of Congress, none of who was mentioned by the other two papers. The *Washington Times* also carried a favorable editorial, as did the *Wall Street Journal.*

There was much to criticize in the TV coverage. All the

networks gave a lot of attention to the claims on Wednesday that the medical students in Grenada were safe and that their safety was a flimsy pretext for the invasion. As soon as the students were brought home to tell their own stories, that was proven to be false. All but one praised the action and expressed their gratitude to the Marines and the Rangers. Both ABC and CBS showed filmed reactions of Cubans in Havana, all of it obviously rehearsed. ABC's "Nightline" gave a lot of time to spokesmen for Havana and Moscow, with commentator George Will permitted an occasional response to their lies and diatribes. Those who stayed with the program until 12:30 A.M. heard the poll results and learned that the people are behind the president. Nothing else on TV would have given them that impression.

November 4, 1983

45

A Message for the Media

The media have been screaming about how terrible it was that reporters were not permitted to accompany the Rangers and Marines on the operation to liberate Grenada from the murderous thugs who had seized control of the island. NBC commentator John Chancellor was almost apoplectic with rage. He said, "The American government is doing whatever it wants to in Grenada without any representative of the American public watching what it's doing."

The fact is that all the Americans in the Grenada operation were representatives and servants of the American people, from the admiral in charge down to the Marine Corps privates. What Chancellor meant was that there were no representatives of the media present. It is not surprising that John Chancellor should equate the media with the American public. Like Louis XIV, our media elite have acquired the habit of thinking that they are the state.

Chancellor and other journalists have said that the press could have been taken along on the operation with no security risk, and some have noted that in World War II our journalists were included in the most sensitive operations, even commando raids.

True, but there was a big difference between the reporters who covered World War II and the present crop. In those long-ago days, the reporters were on our side. They wanted to see the United States and its allies win the war just as much as those of us who were doing the fighting. They wouldn't have considered writing stories that could aid Hitler or the Japanese, either by giving them valuable intelligence or be undermining the will of the American people to fight the war to victory. And even if they tried to do that, they would have had to get through very strict censorship.

All that changed with Vietnam. Jim Lucas, a veteran from World War II, returned from a tour of duty in Vietnam for the Scripps-Howard papers in 1967 to say that the *New York Times* had never had a reporter in Vietnam who was on our side. I reported that to Turner Catledge, then the managing editor of the *Times,* and to my surprise, he didn't dispute it, except to say that you couldn't tell it from their reporting. He was wrong. After the war was lost, James Reston, a top editor and columnist for the *Times,* observed that "maybe the historians will agree that the reporters and cameras were decisive in the end" in forcing "the withdrawal of American power from Vietnam."

Karen DeYoung, the foreign editor of the *Washington Post,* is typical of many of our journalistic elite today. In covering the rebellion in Nicaragua that overthrew Somoza and brought the communists to power, she shamelessly covered up the hard-core communist backgrounds of the Sandinista leaders who had been trained in Cuba. Later, teaching a journalism class at the leftwing Institute for Policy Studies, DeYoung said, "Most journalists now, most Western journalists at least, are very eager to seek out guerrilla groups, leftist groups, because you assume they must be the good guys."

But the security problem doesn't arise only because many journalists (most, according to DeYoung) have leftist sympathies. Some of our top media figures, including Arthur Ochs Sulzberger, the chairman and president of the *New York Times,* are on record as saying that they consider it their duty to ferret out and publish government secrets. *Newsweek* magazine has chided editors who say that they would not run stories exposing secret covert actions by the U.S. government if *they* decided those actions were "necessary, prudent, and moral." That's wrong says *Newsweek*. Run the stories. Don't make moral judgments!

On October 27, all three TV networks aired video tapes of action on Grenada provided by the Pentagon. CBS showed its great displeasure by labeling the pictures, "Cleared by Defense Department Censors," and Dan Rather said twice that they were "shot and censored by the U.S. government." The implication was that they were untrustworthy. But last August 3, CBS News used video tapes shot on the Soviet ship, the Ulyanov, in the Nicaraguan port to prove that President Reagan had been wrong in saying that it was carrying military equipment. Rather didn't mention that the tape was shot by a Cuban camera crew. Such journalists shouldn't be trusted with secrets that can mean life or death for our fighting men.

November 11, 1983

On November 3, CBS hired Grenadians to poll 304 residents of the island. Over 90 percent said they were glad our troops had come, and 85 percent said that they felt our goal had been to "free the people of Grenada from the Cubans." An identical percentage said they had felt they were in danger before our troops landed, and 76 percent thought Cuba was seeking control of their government and 65 percent thought the airport the Cubans were building was for Cuban-Soviet military purposes, not tourism as had been claimed.

Dan Rather and CBS gave this poll what amounted to a quiet burial at 11:30 P.M. on November 4. They reported that over 90 percent welcomed our invasion, that they overwhelmingly agreed that the airport was military, not for tourism, and that most thought the students were in danger. That was it. There was no mention of the belief that we freed them from the Cubans. That was the last heard of that poll on CBS TV news.

November 18, 1983

47

ABC's Nuclear Firestorm

Robert Dornan, a former Republican congressman from California who is now president of the American Space Frontier Committee, has labeled the ABC movie "The Day After," a major propaganda effort by ABC to influence the debate over the deployment of the Pershing II and cruise missiles in Western Europe. Leonard Goldenson, the chairman of the board of ABC, denies this. He says, "This is a motion picture of an *event* without advocacy intention and without postulation. We are making every effort to maintain this objective."

ABC officials have insisted that there is nothing political or propagandistic about the movie, but no one seems to believe them. This came through very clearly in an unusual discussion of the film on the CBS program, "60 Minutes," on November 13. It is unusual for one network to give publicity to an upcoming feature on a rival network, but so great was the firestorm generated by the ABC movie about the destruction of Kansas City by a Soviet nuclear missile that CBS broke the unwritten rule.

Congressman Edward Markey, the Massachusetts Democrat who introduced the nuclear freeze resolution in the House, was shown on "60 Minutes" saying that the movie would help politicize people, making them more dovish. He said that it would help get people elected to Congress who were in tune with Mr. Markey's dovish views on defense, and he pointed out that the switching of a handful of votes would make it possible to vote down the MX missile and many other weapons systems. Markey said ABC should be praised.

Brandon Stoddard, the president of ABC Motion Pictures, insisted when interviewed by "60 Minutes" that this movie had nothing to do with the nuclear freeze movement. He was asked, "Why on earth is the right so irritated at ABC?" He replied, "I think they are as irritated as the left seems to be overjoyed." He was then asked, "If the right is irritated and the left is overjoyed, then how can you, Brandon Stoddard, whose brainchild this was, sit here and insist that it is not a political movie?"

That was very easy for Mr. Stoddard. He simply said, "I'll say again and again that it's not. It was never intended to be, and it isn't." Unfortunately for Mr. Stoddard, the man who wrote the film, Ed Hume, didn't seem to agree. On camera, Hume said that he had "a long sympathy with the disarmament movement" and that when he was asked by ABC to write the movie, he "saw it as a very fortunate coincidence, sort of the right person at the right time." Hume went on to say that he was alarmed by the state of our defense policy, saying, "I think things are out of control. And I'm scared." And so he wrote a script to scare everyone else. But he didn't think it was political to be sympathetic to disarmament.

Hume insisted that ABC asked him to do the movie not knowing what his views were and that he never made the network aware of his thinking. Robert Dornan says he finds that very hard to believe. Dornan says that he has written scripts and been involved in the fights that inevitably occur when there is controversy about what to include and what to take out. He says that in any movie as controversial as "The Day After" there is no way ABC could not have known that in Ed Hume they had a writer sympathetic to the anti-nuclear movement. The director of the film, Nicholas Meyer, had similar sympathies, and it would appear that the ABC executives that he dealt with were of like mind. Meyer has said that while the ABC officials had been "scared" by the criticism of the movie, they were very proud of it and considered it "the most important movie they've ever made."

That would explain why ABC is airing the movie just when the controversy over the deployment of the new missiles in Europe is at it height. It would have been logical for them to delay the airing a few months unless they wanted to do something to help block the deployment of those missiles, a prime Soviet objective. They are also releasing the movie to be shown in West German theaters beginning December 2. An anti-nuclear German said, "By releasing 'The Day After' now, we hope we can change the minds of people in our government about the missiles while there's still time."

November 25, 1983

Fortunately, there was not a lot of gore to show. Only sixteen Americans died in the operation. We mourned their deaths. They were not just statistics. They gave their lives unselfishly to accomplish the mission that had been assigned to them. The main story in Grenada was that the mission was carried out successfully.

The 600 American students who were rescued and the Grenadian people who were liberated from their Cuban-dominated masters were delighted. The great majority of the American people were also highly pleased. Chancellor and his colleagues were angry because they hadn't been allowed to tarnish this success by graphically exploiting on TV the deaths of those who gave their lives to help bring it about.

December 2, 1983

◉ 49

Killing With Silence

Years ago, one of the prominent Hollywood writers who was a member of the Communist Party, wrote an article in a party magazine to defend the Communists in the movie industry against the criticism that they were not getting enough pro-communist films made. He granted that there was some validity to the criticism, but he pointed out how successful he and his colleagues had been in preventing the production of anti-communist movies. He cited a number of best selling books with anti-communist messages that had never been made into movies, including Victor Kravchenko's *I Chose Freedom* and Jan Valtin's *Out of the Night.*

That was 40 years ago. Although much has been learned about the horrors of communism in the Soviet Union, Eastern Europe, China, Cambodia, Vietnam and Cuba in the meantime, the only thing that seems to have changed is that it is now harder for an anti-communist book to get published. Anti-communist movies are still scarce as hen's teeth. None of the comrades has taken credit for this publicly, but it is obvious that there is nothing accidental about it.

In September, a first-rate British movie, "The Final Op-

 50

Media Reaction to Public Outrage

Our news media were taken very much by surprise when the public failed to respond as expected to their complaints about having been excluded from the Grenada rescue operation for two days. "Where is the Outrage?" asked the Poughkeepsie Journal, disappointed that the public had not rallied to endorse the complaints against the government that had been voiced by Dan Rather, John Chancellor and others.

The outrage was there, but it was not directed against the government, but against those in the media who were complaining. Chancellor, the NBC commentator, was deluged with mail, and he found it running eight to one against him. This stunned many in the media, and columns and commentary began appearing lamenting the public's lack of appreciation of the media's role in our society. One such column was headlined, "Sorry, folks, but you're wrong." That typified the most common response. There was precious little tendency to ask, "Is it possible that we in the media have gotten on the wrong track and what should we do about it?" The more common reaction was to bemoan the public ignorance and suggest the need to cd-ucate the people.

But there have been a few notable exceptions. The December 12 issue of *Time* magazine devoted its cover story to the growing criticism of the media. The article began with this summary of the criticism: "They are rude and accusatory, cynical and almost unpatriotic. They twist facts to suit their not-so-hidden liberal agenda. They meddle in politics, harass business, invade people's privacy, and then walk off without regard to the pain and chaos they leave behind. They are arrogant and self-righteous, brushing aside most criticism as the uninformed carping of cranks and ideologues. To top it off, they claim that their behavior is sanctioned, indeed sanctified, by the U.S. Constitution."

Time noted that the hostile public reaction to media criticism of Grenada was related to a perception that "journalists regard themselves as utterly detached from and perhaps even hostile to, the government of their country." It pointed out that a poll taken by the National Opinion Research Center had revealed a sharp decline in public confidence in the press since 1976. Only 13.7 percent of those who responded in 1983 indicated that they had a great deal of confidence in the press. That was down from 29 percent in 1976.

What has happened to bring about this change? *Time* listed some of the factors—the attention given to the libel suits filed by Gen. William Westmoreland and Dr. Carl Galloway against CBS, the fake story about an eight-year-old heroin addict that won a Pulitzer Prize for the *Washington Post,* and the excessive prying into people's private lives. It also delved into the more deep-rooted cause of the problem—the heavy domination of Big Media by writers and editors who are far to the left of the average American in their political and social views.

This has been documented by surveys, the most notable being the Lichter-Rothman survey of the views of 240 "media elite," the reporters and editors who staff the big papers, news magazines, wire services and TV networks. *Time* mentioned this survey, but it didn't cite what I consider its most revealing finding: that 81 percent of this elite group voted for George McGovern for president in 1972.

As liberal bias has come to mean hostility to a strong national defense, sympathy for Cuban-backed terrorists, and tears for murderers faced with execution, the public has become progressively disenchanted with the liberal media. Robert Kendall, editor of the Martinsville, Indiana *Reporter* put it this way: "The people who dominate my trade are divorcing themselves from the country's best interests and from its people; and that's bad, and not just for business."

That being the root of the problem, the answer would seem obvious: correct the imbalance and hire more journalists who are in tune with the mainstream of America. But even *Time* magazine could not bring itself to face up to that simple conclusion.

December 16, 1983

51

Juicy Secret FBI Files Downplayed

A story of scandals in Democratic administrations from Franklin D. Roosevelt to Lyndon Johnson that make Watergate look like a Sunday school picnic were brought to light in the December 19, 1983 issue of *U. S. News & World Report*, Victor Lasky, author of *It Didn't Start With Watergate* and biographer of both John F. Kennedy and Robert Kennedy, says the material is "dynamite." It comes from heretofore secret FBI files that were under the personal control of the late J. Edgar Hoover because of their highly sensitive nature. Some 7,000 pages from these files were recently released under a Freedom of Information request.

The most sensational story these files have brought to light is an explanation of the sudden decimation of the Army Counterintelligence Corps (CIC) in 1944, at the height of World War II. According to military documents that were recently declassified, the wartime head of the CIC had told an army historian in 1953 that his organization had been nearly ruined because its agents had uncovered "something that would be personally embarrassing to the Roosevelt family." The just-released FBI documents reveal what that "something" was.

The CIC had under surveillance an Army Air Corps sergeant, Joseph Lash, who had been very active in leftist movements. According to a memo in the FBI files, two Army colonels had told an FBI agent that the CIC had bugged a hotel room in Urbana, IL and had recorded a sexual encounter between Sgt. Lash and the wife of the President of the United States, Eleanor Roosevelt. Lash had become acquainted with the Roosevelts through his political activity.

The memo relates that this recording was played for FDR by two top Army intelligence officers at a White House session that lasted from 10:00 p.m. until dawn. Mrs. Roosevelt was called in, and a terrific fight ensued. At 5:00 a.m., FDR summoned General Arnold, Chief of the Army Air Corps, and ordered him to ship Lash out of the country to a combat post within 10 hours. Lash and 10 other airmen were abruptly pulled out of a school they were attending and shipped to the South Pacific. The FBI memo goes on to say that it was subsequently learned that FDR had ordered that anyone who knew anything about this case should be "immediately...sent to the South Pacific for action against the Japs until they were killed."

U. S. News & World Report describes this as "a third-hand account," suggesting that it might lack credibility. However, former FBI Special Agent George C. Burton, who wrote the memo on December 31, 1943, says that he had no doubt about the credibility of his sources. At the time, Burton was responsible for liaison between the FBI and all other intelligence agencies. It was his business to find out what was happening to the Army Counterintelligence Corps, and his memo was written for the information of the director of the FBI. It was not the retelling of idle gossip.

That Sgt. Lash was immediately sent overseas and that the CIC was virtually dismantled are undisputed facts. The Army's ability to investigate subversives in its ranks was severely crippled, and when Gen. Eisenhower requested CIC personnel to support the invasion of Normandy, the Army had great difficulty in filling that urgent request. Roosevelt had unquestionably played fast and loose with national security. The only reason to doubt that it was done to cover up his wife's infidelity is Joseph Lash's insistence that sex was not involved in his friendship with Mrs. Roosevelt.

Lash discussed these charges and even printed Burton's 1943 memo in his book, *Love, Eleanor*, which was published in 1982. Surprisingly, the affair was virtually ignored by the media then, and most of our national media seem intent on burying it even now. Not one word about all this was mentioned on any of the network television news programs. The *New York Times* carried a story about the newly released FBI files. It was buried on page A19, and there was no mention at all of the Roosevelts. The *Washington Post* put the story on page A14 under the headline, "Secret Hoover Files Show Misuse of FBI." It discussed this case, but clearly Franklin and Eleanor Roosevelt still enjoy the protection of Big Media.

December 23, 1983

Note: After this column was published I heard from a former Air Corps officer who had been involved in the surveillance of Joseph Lash. He said this turned up no evidence that the meeting between Lash and Mrs. Roosevelt, which took place in Chicago, involved sex. He believes the matter came to the attention of the president as a result of the hotel manager's having reported the surveillance, not because of any initiative taken by the CIC. He believes the repercussions on the CIC were less severe than the FBI report indicated.

52

Which Side is "Our" Side?

A few weeks after the Grenada rescue operation, addressing the annual convention of the Society of Professional Journalists, I defended the decision not to permit reporters to accompany the assault forces. Taking note of the fact that reporters had been in on all the big operations in World War II, I pointed out that one of the big differences then was that all the reporters were clearly on our side.

One of the first questions I was asked by a young journalist in the audience was, "When you say the reporters were on our side, which side do you mean?" The question took me by surprise. I thought that perhaps the questioner didn't know who we fought in World War II. My answer was simply, "The American side."

Shortly after that I recounted this incident to a somewhat older reporter who was interviewing me for a television program. Her reaction stunned me. After a momentary pause, she said, "That was going to be my next question."

"What's going on here?" I wondered. Have we gone so

181

far that the meaning of "our side" in wartime is unclear?

Then along came Secretary of State George Shultz. During a press interview on December 15, Mr. Shultz defended the brief exclusion of reporters from Grenada in terms similar to those I had used a month earlier. In World War II, he said, "reporters were involved all along. And on the whole, they were on our side." He went a little further than I had gone, saying that now "it seems as though reporters are always against us. . . . They're always seeking to report something that's going to screw things up."

Five days later, President Reagan held a news conference, and Sam Donaldson, the ABC White House correspondent, asked him if he agreed with that statement by Mr. Shultz.

The president replied: "I'm simply going to say that I do believe, Sam, that sometimes, beginning with the Korean conflict and certainly in the Vietnam conflict, there was more criticizing of our own forces and what we were trying to do, to the point that it didn't seem that there was much criticism being leveled on the enemy. And sometimes I just wish that we could get together on what is of importance to our national security in a situation of that kind, what is endangering our forces, and what is helping them in their mission."

Donaldson then asked: "Well, sir, is one of the problems a definition of the word 'us'? When Secretary Shultz uses it, or if you say 'our forces,' do you think he was using it in terms of an administration, the Reagan administration?"

"No," said President Reagan.

"Or," persisted Donaldson, "let's say, the Carter administration? In other words, is 'us' the administration in power, or is there a higher duty that the press has?"

The president replied: "I thought the us he was talking about was our side, militarily—in other words, all of America."

This time the questioner was one of the nation's top television correspondents. Not only does he cover the White House for ABC, but he also appears regularly as a kind of commentator on ABC's Sunday morning program, "This Week," with David Brinkley. I find it ominous that a journalist of his stature, like the youngster at the SPJ convention, doesn't understand the meaning of "our side" when our country is fighting a war.

I don't recall anyone during World War II portraying that massive national effort as a project of "the Roosevelt administration." The change that has taken place among journalists like Donaldson since then is evidently not simply that they are not on our side, but they don't even recognize that there is such a thing as the American side. Oldtimers like Ronald Reagan and George Shultz don't understand that. And neither do most of the American people, whose reaction to *our* victory in Grenada was a media defeat.

December 30, 1983